THE MARCHANTS AVIZO

BY

I[OHN] B[ROWNE,] *Marchant*,

1589

THE
MARCHANTS AVIZO

BY

I[OHN] B[ROWNE,] *Marchant*,

1589

EDITED BY

PATRICK McGRATH

DEPARTMENT OF HISTORY,

UNIVERSITY OF BRISTOL

PUBLISHED BY THE

BAKER LIBRARY, HARVARD GRADUATE SCHOOL

OF BUSINESS ADMINISTRATION

SOLDIERS FIELD, BOSTON 63

MASSACHUSETTS, U.S.A.

Publication Number 11 of
The Kress Library of Business and Economics

PRINTED AT THE
HARVARD UNIVERSITY PRINTING OFFICE
CAMBRIDGE, MASSACHUSETTS, U. S. A.

INTRODUCTION

IN the year after the defeat of the Armada, there was published in London a little handbook entitled *The Marchants Avizo*. It was the work of an experienced Bristol merchant, John Browne, who seems to have been the first to realize the desirability of providing young men just starting their commercial careers with a manual of information and advice on the problems they would meet when they undertook the responsible task of acting as agents for their masters in foreign countries. This little vade-mecum of some seventy pages was a handy work of reference to the complicated currencies of Portugal, Spain, and France; it provided its readers with a number of model letters on which to base their correspondence; it showed them how to keep simple accounts; and it furnished them with illustrations of the business documents they would meet in the course of their trade. Nor was the author concerned simply with business technique. He had a good deal to say about the religious practices and moral standards required from a young merchant. *The Marchants Avizo* is thus of considerable interest, not only because it is one of the earliest books of its kind, but because it throws light on the training of a young business man in the later sixteenth century, and because it helps the reader in some measure to understand the general outlook of a merchant in Elizabethan England.

THE AUTHOR AND HIS CAREER

On the title pages of all the editions of *The Marchants Avizo*, the author's identity is concealed under the pseudonym 'I. B. Marchant,' and in the editions issued after 1591 there is no other indication of the writer's name. But for the evidence of the editions of 1589, 1590, and 1591, which were unknown until comparatively recently, there would be considerable doubt as to who wrote the book, for in later sixteenth century Bristol there were at least half a dozen merchants with the initials J. B.,[1] and some of them were, to all appearances, well qualified to produce such a work. Lt. Colonel Bramble, who

[1] The capital "I" was commonly used for "J", and it can easily be shown that in *The Marchants Avizo* "I. B." in fact represents the modern "J. B."

was familiar only with the edition of 1607, suggested that the author was John Barker, and, on internal evidence alone, it would be possible to make out a strong case, for John Barker's name appears in the book, and he was a prominent merchant who was in 1583 treasurer of the Company of Merchants trading to Spain and Portugal, countries with which *The Marchants Avizo* is particularly concerned. Fortunately, the matter is settled by the dedication appearing in the editions of 1589, 1590, and 1591. This begins as follows: 'To the Worshipfvl Maister Thomas Aldworth Marchant of Bristowe . . . your bounded in good will John Browne, wisheth vnto your worships, felicitie in heaven and prosperitie in earth.' It is not clear why in the editions after 1591 the name of John Browne was replaced simply by the initials, but we can at least be grateful that the earlier versions furnish the answer to the problem of authorship and make it unnecessary to canvas the rival claims of other J. B.'s.

The task of pinning down the John Browne who wrote *The Marchants Avizo* is made easier by the fact that among the burgesses of later sixteenth century Bristol there were few who bore this name, and of these only two were merchants. The choice in fact lies between the John Browne who was mayor of Bristol in 1572 and his son John Browne, who was baptized on 3 August 1559. The elder John Browne was apprenticed in 1538. If we assume that he was not under twelve years of age when he entered his apprenticeship, he would have been in his early sixties in 1589, the year in which *The Marchants Avizo* was first published. At that time, his son, John Browne the younger, was just over thirty. We cannot entirely exclude the possibility that the younger John Browne wrote the book, but it seems unlikely, for the work appears to be that of an experienced and mature merchant. Moreover, as we shall see, there is evidence suggesting that *The Marchants Avizo* was put together some years before 1589, when the younger Browne was still in the very early stages of his career. Finally, if he was the author, we might have expected him to indicate this in some way, so that people would not give the credit to his father, as they would otherwise naturally tend to do.

The author of *The Marchants Avizo* came from a Bristol family which had been important in the Spanish trade from at least the early sixteenth century. He was the son of yet another John Browne, a Bristol draper. John Browne the draper was already dead when on

10 September 1538 his son was apprenticed to a Bristol merchant, William Spratt. The apprenticeship was for twelve years, but it is probable that the apprentice did not serve the full term, for apprentices were not allowed to marry and yet we know that on 14 February 1546 John Browne married Margaret Cooke in the church of St. Nicholas in Bristol. The first child was born on 6 February 1547 and was christened Roger after his maternal grandfather, Roger Cooke, merchant and alderman of Bristol, but he did not live long. Child mortality was high in the sixteenth century, and of the six children of the marriage only John and Alice were still alive when their father made his will in 1595.

Little is known of John Browne's early career as a merchant, but it appears from his book that while he was still an apprentice he went to Spain and Portugal in his master's service and experienced the need for a guide of the kind he was later to set about compiling.

Although the Burgess Books of Bristol do not tell us when John Browne first took up the freedom as a merchant, we may assume that it was some time late in 1545 or early in 1546. Possibly his father-in-law, who was a prominent merchant, gave him a helping hand in the early stages of his career. The young man must have established himself in business fairly quickly and shown ability as a man of affairs, for in September 1558 he was chosen one of the two sheriffs. Possibly he was by that time already a member of the Common Council of the City, that exclusive group of just over forty members in whose hands was concentrated complete control of municipal affairs. Among his colleagues on the Council was Thomas Aldworth, the distinguished merchant to whom *The Marchants Avizo* was principally dedicated.

In 1572, John Browne was chosen mayor of Bristol. *Adams's Chronicle of Bristol* states: 'This mayor kept the like watches on those nights (Midsummer Day and St. Peter's Night) but turned the same into a general muster in warlike sort; and all the burgesses being fully armed with all sorts of warlike weapons, every craft and science several by themselves with their drums and colours, which was well used and made a comely show.' It goes on to record: 'Also this mayor caused a reformation to be made for the measures of barrels and kinterkins, which were made larger and of a bigger size than before.' The mayor's interest in military affairs is seen in the formidable list of weapons he bequeathed to his son, and the reforms he carried out in the measures of barrels and kilderkins were possibly a reflection of that interest in weights and measures which he displays in the pages of *The Marchants Avizo.*

The municipal account books known as *The Mayor's Audits* throw some light on events during John Browne's mayoralty. There were the usual diversions of Elizabethan Bristol. We learn that the Earl of Worcester's players, the Earl of Sussex's players, and the Earl of Essex's players, all visited the city and received payment for performing before the mayor and aldermen, but we are not told which plays they performed. Six shillings and eight pence were given to 'my lord of Leycestres bereward for bayting his beares before mr mayer and thaldermen.' John Browne's interest in the amenities of his native city is perhaps reflected in the statement that ten young elm trees were set up in the marsh 'by the commandement of mr mayer.'

The chief magistrate had also to deal with weightier matters. Public policy in Elizabethan England required local authorities to make some effort to see that adequate food supplies were available at a reasonable price, and in 1572 the city chamberlain and his man were sent to London by the command of the mayor and aldermen to procure a letter from the Lord Treasurer 'for the staying of 2 trowes of corne and to have ordre to sell yt in the market.' On another occasion, the great religious controversies of the time had their local repercussions when a pursuivant came down from London with a proclamation 'touching the calling in of the bokes named the admonytion to the parliament.' It has been said of this work that it marked the definite adoption by some of the puritans of a Presbyterian platform and therefore of a revolutionary policy, and the government was very anxious to suppress it. It would be interesting to know whether the mayor secured any copies and, if so, what he made of the book, but the record merely states that the pursuivant was given five shillings.

Other duties which fell to the mayor during his term of office included the entertaining of the celebrated Mr. Toby Mathew, who preached three sermons at St. Mary Redcliffe in Whitsun week. John Browne was paid ten shillings for the cost of the preacher's three dinners. Another pleasant official occasion was the holding of the

Bristol Admiralty Court, when there was expended 'for i gallon of claret xvid, for i gallon secke ijs and for iiij ^{lbs} of sugar iiij ^{s} geven to mr mayer that day according to custome.'

The Mayor's Audits contain a large number of John Browne's signatures from 1561 to 1594. The frequency with which John Browne's services were required as one of the auditors suggests that his ability was held in high esteem by his fellow councillors. It may be noted that he was often associated in this work with Thomas Aldworth.

John Browne's son was admitted to the freedom of Bristol on 23 August 1582. It was possibly for the use of this son that his father originally compiled *The Marchants Avizo*, which, he states, at first he had 'onely made priuate for instruction of me and mine.'

A man of wealth and ability like John Browne was so obviously fitted for the responsibilities and expenses of the office of mayor that he was in danger of having the position thrust upon him more than once. Evidently by the middle fifteen-eighties John Browne was no longer willing to undertake the heavy task, and perhaps he felt that he needed all his spare time for writing. Some such explanation no doubt lies behind the entry in *The Mayor's Audits* for 22 September 1585–6: 'Received of Mr. John Browne Alderman the somme of xx^{li} in monney which he giveth to the Mayor and Comminaltie with xj peces of Ordynance, viz. vj Fawkenettes of yren with their carriages, and fyve small Rabnettes of brasse, In consideracion whereof he is by the Consennt of Mr Mayor thaldermen and the whole common counsell for ever hereafter dicharged of thoffice of Mayraltie of this cittie. I saie received in monney xx^{li}.'

John Browne's little book appeared in 1589, and the author lived for six years after publication. His will is dated in June 1595, and although it does not tell us anything about *The Marchants Avizo*, it is one of the main sources for our knowledge of its author. From it we learn that John Browne was married to Margaret Cooke, daughter of the late alderman Roger Cooke. She was still alive when the will was drawn up and had two surviving children, John and Alice. John Browne the younger was married and had four children, William, Thomas, Jeremiah, and Grace. Alice was married to John Roberts and lived with her husband, according to Browne, 'in the backer part of my house.'

Like many merchants of the time, John Browne had a good deal of capital invested in property in Bristol. His bequests included 'the fee simple of my dwelling house upon the back . . . ,' 'two tenements with the sellers underneath them' in Marsh Street, a tenement in Wine Street and a garden in Redcross Street. In addition, he left 'my gret house upon the back where my father in law dwelt,' 'the next house adjoining the aforesaid great house,' and a tenement in fee simple in the Weir. There was also a certain amount of leasehold property.

Various bequests of money amounted to a little over £400, and his wife was given an annuity of £18 payable for a term of years by the corporation of Bristol. The will mentions in some detail much furniture, plate, and household stuff including 'my silver basen and yore of percell gilt wainge 66 ounces,' 'one dozen of Spoones with Apostells heddes wainge 14 ounces,' and 'my great Venis chest and a greate Ellen Chest which lieth att my Chamber dore.'

In an age when private citizens might be required to take up arms to deal with civil disturbances or with invasion from abroad, it is not surprising to find weapons in the house of a peaceful merchant, and John Browne seems to have been particularly well equipped to deal with any emergency. He left to his son 'all my Armor, that is to say, Corslett of proofe, Targett of proofe, ij muskettes, v Callivers, xij staves or halbertes, certen hedpeaces, a corslett for a pickman, with all other Armor and furniture therto belonginge.'

It is often dangerous to deduce the character of a man from the terms of his will. The expression of religious beliefs appearing in such documents may be merely the conventional forms of the time, but the tone of this will tends to confirm the impression given in *The Marchants Avizo* that John Browne took his religion seriously. In addition, we gather that he was a kindly and thoughtful man. He made suitable provision for the welfare and comfort of his widow, and arranged that his daughter and son-in-law should continue to enjoy the use of 'the backer part of my house' until another lease fell in and accommodation could be provided for them elsewhere. He left a legacy to provide 'good strong shirts and smocks . . . to be given to the poore men and weomen of the Almehouse in the Marshe and to others that are the most needfull poor of the said parish.' Thirteen shillings a year was left to help pay for repairs to the church of St. Nicholas, in which parish John Browne lived and in the crypt of which he desired to be buried. Twelve poor men and twelve poor women were to be provided with gowns and headgear by his overseers 'before my departinge from the worlde.' Three days after he had signed the will, the testator had some after-thoughts and added a codicil in which he made a number of bequests to friends 'for a token of my love and goodwill.'

On 14 July 1595, John Browne was buried in the crypt of St. Nicholas's Church as he had desired. No monument has survived, but *The Marchants Avizo* gives him a more enduring claim to remembrance than stone or marble.

BRISTOL AND THE TRADE WITH SPAIN AND PORTUGAL IN THE LATER SIXTEENTH CENTURY

The author of *The Marchants Avizo* was mainly concerned with the Spanish and Portuguese trades. He does, it is true, say a little about the currency and the weights and measures in France; but he does not mention Ireland, in spite of its very important commerce with Bristol; and most of his illustrations refer to business relations with the Iberian peninsula. He was probably drawing to a considerable extent on his personal experience, and the Spanish and Portuguese trades were in any case of special significance in the life of Bristol and, indeed, of the whole country.

'The trade with Spain,' wrote the Spanish ambassador in 1580, 'is of the greatest importance to the English . . . it being the principal source of their wealth and strength. . . They have no other trade as profitable, both on account of the vast sums of specie they bring, which they can get from no other place, and the richness of the merchandise which they carry.' In 1586 a Spanish agent in England remarked: 'They are much troubled with this war which they have entered into against Spain as the whole country is without trade, and knows not how to recover it, the shipping and commerce here being much dependent upon communications with Spain and Portugal.' The note to the first verse of the poem in *The Marchants Avizo* referring to the 'long stay of the Marchantes trade to the great decay of many a one' is some indication of the importance of this trade in the eyes of Bristolians, for the severe commercial depression of 1586–87 was in considerable measure due to the diminished trade with Spain and her dependencies; and the effects of the crisis were particularly severe in the west country.

During the reign of Elizabeth I, this trade was subjected to interruptions from time to time, even before war broke out, but at the period when *The Marchants Avizo* was probably compiled, the position was reasonably satisfactory. From 1573 relations between England and Spain improved considerably, and in 1576 a treaty between England and Portugal patched up for a time the disputes between the two countries. Even the conquest of Portugal by Spain in 1580 did not interrupt the trade, for although Elizabeth I was willing on occasions to give support to the Portuguese pretender, Don Antonio, this did not interfere seriously with commercial relations. In 1584 Philip II agreed to the appointment of an Englishman as consul in Lisbon and confirmed the privileges of English merchants there. So important was the trade in the eyes of English merchants that even after 1585 efforts were made to continue it in some measure by various clandestine channels.

In 1577, Elizabeth I, pursuing the Tudor policy of favouring 'a well-ordered trade,' issued letters-patent giving a monopoly of the Spanish and Portuguese trades to members of a newly formed Spanish Company. The foundation members included certain courtiers and officials, over 200 members from London, and 173 merchants from other ports. The importance of the trade to Bristol is reflected in the fact that 76 of these provincial members were Bristolians, and the city supplied three of the forty Assistants, one of whom was Thomas Aldworth. The Bristol members were of course subject to the general regulations of the Company, which had its headquarters in London, but they seem to have formed a local branch with its own officials and accounts. It is not certain what relationship this branch bore to the Society of Merchant Venturers of Bristol, which had received its charter in 1552, but certainly no Bristolian could legally trade with Spain or Portugal unless he belonged to the Spanish Company. The record of the apprenticeship of Robert Aldworth specifically states that his master was 'one of the Society of merchants trading to Spain and Portugal,' and there are a number of similar entries even for the period after England had drifted into open war with Spain.

The nature of the trade between England and the Iberian peninsula is described at some length in a document known as *A special Direction for Divers trades* which was probably written by a west country merchant about 1575–85. Commodities sent from England to all parts of Galicia included 'course cloth and Bridgwaters, northern halfe clothes, manchester cottons, hides, calf skins, sheepe skins, dressed breaknocks, bristowe frises and tynbye frizes, waxe, flaninge and wedmoles of Wales, wheate, Butter, chease, highe cotton fryses of carmarthen in Sowthe Wales.' In return came wine, oranges and lemons, and timber. Andalusia took hides, calf skins, kersies, lead, tin, pipe staves, copper, bell metal and other goods, and sent back salt, oils, raisins, silks, cochineal, indigo, cordovan skins, shumack and soap. To Lisbon Englishmen exported butter, cheese, and fine cloth of Bristol and of Somerset, and received in exchange oil, salt, soap, calicoes, spices and other East India produce. Bayona in Galicia and Oporto in Portugal received similar goods to those sent to Lisbon, and returned oranges, lemons, and great onions. Bilbao and San Sebastian imported hides, calf skins, and Somerset cloth from Shepton Mallet, Bridgwater and Taunton, and exported iron, oil, pitch, sugar, liquorice, sword blades and other goods.

The Iberian trade, then, was of great value to English merchants, and Bristol was particularly well placed to play an important part in it. The geographical situation of the city enabled it to act as a collecting and distributing centre for the produce of a wide hinterland, and through it went a great deal of the trade both of Wales and of Ireland. In the eyes of Bristol merchants of the later sixteenth century the Spanish and Portuguese markets were all the more important because government policy placed restrictions on trade with other countries. It is true Bristolians also dealt with Ireland and with France, but they were specifically excluded by the Bristol Merchant Venturers' charters from the great English cloth market in the Netherlands and North Germany, and from 1581 onwards the Levant trade was increasingly coming under the control of Londoners.

The Marchants Avizo was to a considerable extent designed to show young men their way about when they first went overseas to countries which were, or at any rate had been up to the outbreak of war, the chief foreign markets for Bristol merchants.

THE DEVELOPMENT OF THE BOOK

Although William Norton did not register *The Marchants Avizo* until 3 October 1589, the author had clearly been compiling his book for some time before he thought of publishing it. He states in the dedication that it was only 'upon verie earnest motion & persuasion of a friend' that he decided 'to set foorth in publick this matter, which I onely had made priuate for instruction of me and mine.' Now John Browne's son had not become a freeman of Bristol until 1582, and was probably learning the business as an apprentice or servant during the period 1575–82. It may well be that the book was based on material which his father provided for his instruction during those years.

It should also be noted that most of the accounts and letters in *The Marchants Avizo* concern the dealings of Thomas Aldworth and his servant 'R. A.' who was clearly not a fully fledged merchant at the time when the documents were written. It is reasonable to assume that 'R. A.' was Robert Aldworth, the nephew and apprentice of Thomas Aldworth. Robert Aldworth became his uncle's apprentice on 20 April 1577 and was not admitted to the freedom of Bristol as a merchant until 10 December 1584. If we can assume that the letters and documents relating to R. A. are edited copies of those actually sent to him or written by him, we can put the date of at least part of the book between 1577 and 1584.

There is no reference in *The Marchants Avizo* to the union of the crowns of Spain and Portugal in 1580 or to the rapid deterioration of Anglo-Spanish relations from 1585. It is true that a note to the first verse of the poem refers indirectly to the effects of the political situation on the state of trade in 1587, but apart from that the author gives no indication that trade was in any way disturbed. His failure to mention events that must have been causing great concern to all engaged in the Spanish trade might, of course, be explained by the fact that he obviously did not want to say anything that would give offence abroad. The omission of any comment on unpleasant political developments might be due to his caution and his tact. On the other hand, if the greater part of the book was in fact compiled some time in the later seventies or early eighties of the sixteenth century, no such explanation is necessary, for trade between England and the Iberian peninsula was then relatively undisturbed.

When John Browne began to consider what kind of material would be helpful to young merchants learning their business, his thoughts probably turned first of all to letters, accounts, and business documents. For this purpose, he might have used his imagination to construct useful examples, or he might have selected and edited some of his own business records. What in fact he seems to have done is to make use of business documents belonging to his friend Thomas Aldworth. We cannot, of course, be quite certain of this, but the letters and other documents in *The Marchants Avizo* do seem to have the flavour of genuine business records, and the names of some of the ships and the initials of some of the people seem to correspond to real ships and real people in Elizabethan Bristol. This may also explain why so many of the documents are signed with the initials 'T. A.' and 'R. A.' rather than with those of John Browne or his apprentice. It would also add point to John Browne's remark in the Dedication: 'Mine own labour or skill I confesse, is but very little or nothing in this thing, because I myselfe do but only as a poore willing labourer, to helpe forwards that worke, the foundation & platforme wherof, is setled and builded alreadie.'

The foundation of *The Marchants Avizo* may thus be some of the Aldworth papers. John Browne possibly selected what he needed, edited them, and gave them the dates which they now bear. To this he added the material relating to weights, measures, and currency which would be quite familiar to him from his own mercantile activities; and he could draw on his own knowledge and experience for the directions he gave for judging the qualities of the various commodities in which the young merchant was likely to trade. For the section of his work entitled 'Certaine godly sentences, necessary for a youth to meditate upon' and for the instructions concerning religious conduct and morality, John Browne could make use of contemporary literature and sermons as well as his own experience of life; and he may have tried his hand as a poet and as a story teller in order to produce the verses at the beginning of the book and the 'profitable and delightful history' at the end. The verses were written not earlier than 1587, and the dedication was dated at his house in

Bristol on 26 October 1589. A publisher had already been found, for William Norton had registered the work with the Stationers' Company in London three weeks earlier. Possibly John Browne had some personal contact with his publisher, for William Norton was the son of Andrew Norton of Bristol. And thus this interesting compilation, which had hitherto been known only to a limited circle in Bristol, was made available to a wider public. The Spanish word *avizo*, meaning information, or warning, was appropriately included in the title of the book.

THE MARCHANTS AVIZO IN RELATION TO THE TRAINING OF A YOUNG MERCHANT IN THE LATER SIXTEENTH CENTURY

A recent work by Dr. Gordon Connell-Smith has thrown a great deal of light on the organization of Anglo-Spanish trade in the early Tudor period and on the part played in it by that much-neglected character, the factor. Most of the factors were commission agents taking for their pains a 'provision' of 2½ per cent. Dr. Connell-Smith thinks that many merchants found it advantageous to employ established merchants with experience of Spanish business methods and with good connections in Spain to handle merchandise on a commission basis, but that nevertheless some of them did send their sons, and even promising young men of little experience, to Spain as factors. He gives a number of illustrations including the 'rake's progress' of Robert Harvey, a young Plymouth lad sent to Spain and Portugal 'to lerne the ffashyon and maner of those parties in the cowrse of marchandise.' Harvey was alleged to have spent his time drinking both on board ship and at the various ports of call, and, owing to his own carelessness and neglect, the money which he had obtained from the sale of his master's goods was stolen. Not all young men were equally irresponsible, and it seems to have been the practice for merchants in Bristol to entrust a great deal of business to them. It was for such young men rather than for the experienced commission agent that *The Marchants Avizo* was intended. It was addressed primarily to factors who were still in their apprenticeship and who were going abroad for the first time in the service of their masters.

Very little is known from other sources about the early training of these budding merchants in Elizabethan Bristol. Most of the young men came of fairly well-to-do families and presumably received some kind of general education before they became apprentices. Probably many of them attended Bristol Grammar School, but we cannot be certain because no early registers of the school have survived.

The period of apprenticeship lasted for at least seven years, but frequently the youth was bound for an even longer time. The earliest age at which he could become a freeman was twenty-one. It is possible that merchants preferred their apprentices to begin their service at a rather later age than was usual in the case of artisans and manual workers. Robert Aldworth, it may be noted, was already 16½ years old when he was apprenticed to his uncle on 27 April 1577. We do not know what kind of education he had received before he embarked on his commercial career, but he may have been to school in London, where his father, Richard Aldworth, was a merchant of importance. Robert was bound apprentice for a period of ten years, but in fact he was allowed to take up the freedom of Bristol on 10 December 1584 when he had served only a little over 7½ years. He was by that time twenty-four years of age.

It may reasonably be assumed that the merchant's apprentice would first of all be taught something of the merchant's art in his master's house, where he would have opportunities of familiarizing himself with the business techniques of the time and of learning something about the commodities in which he was to deal. Then, if he was a promising young man and had got on well, he might be sent to act as his master's agent abroad. This period of experience overseas was invaluable. It gave the young man knowledge and self-confidence, and his early ventures would serve as a test to show whether he had the character and ability to succeed in what was by no means an easy profession. In the words of John Wheeler, secretary to the Society of Merchant Adventurers of England, it enabled him 'to learn good fashions, and to gain experience and knowledge in trade and the manners of strange nations, the better to know the world betimes.'

These business trips abroad had yet another advantage from the point of view of the apprentice. His main task was to carry out commercial transactions on behalf of his master, but it appears from *The Marchants Avizo* that he received on each transaction a 'prouision' or commission of 2½ per cent. In addition, he might, with his master's consent, carry out certain ventures on his own account, probably with capital supplied by his family or friends. He was also allowed, again with his master's permission, to earn commissions by acting as agent for other merchants. Thus, he had considerable opportunities for building up the capital he would require when he eventually set up on his own. We know that in the next century there were excellent possibilities for young men to make money in this way and that London merchants demanded very heavy premiums for those apprentices whom they intended to send overseas. That the prospects were reasonably good in the later sixteenth century, we can gather from the fact that the author of *The Marchants Avizo* insisted that his apprentice must show him the accounts for ventures he made on his own and must not undertake too much work for others lest his master's interests should suffer.

The young man embarking on his first ventures abroad thus had the chance of rendering good service both to his master and to himself, but he must be well trained if he was to fulfil his mission successfully. One of the most important tools of his trade was the efficient handling of correspondence. We may assume that he would have learnt something of this in his master's office and that he would be familiar with his master's Letter Books, but judging from the tone of *The Marchants Avizo*, some young men must have wasted a great deal of time either wondering what to say or laboriously scratching away with their quills in order to produce lengthy epistles full of irrelevancies. It is true that there were becoming increasingly available in the second half of the sixteenth century a number of books containing model letters, but there was nothing as yet specially designed to meet the needs of young businessmen. After the publication of *The Marchants Avizo*, they had only to turn to its eight model letters to find something suitable to most, if not all, of their occasions, and, Angel Day, author of *The English Secretorie*, considered the work 'most fully and amplie suffizing' for instructing a servant or factor on how to address his master — as Miss Jean Robertson has pointed out.[1] It is to be hoped that the young men did not

[1] The first part of the *English Secretorie* appeared in 1586, the second in 1592. In Part II Angel Day stated: "In writing of the last letter, there was shewed me by the Printer, a book called *The Marchants Avizo* helping and in mine opinion most fully and amplie suffizing in this instruction."

take undue advantage of the phrase 'Little newes I heare worth the writing' and that they did not ignore the subsequent instruction 'Here write your news if you have any.'

One of the points on which *The Marchants Avizo* lays great stress is the need for the servant to keep his master well informed both of the progress of his ventures and of the state of the market abroad. If the ship was held up in port by contrary winds, the master must straightway be told. As soon as it reached its destination, a letter must be despatched by the first vessel returning to England. Such information was vital 'because it is the thing euerie Marchant doth especially long after to vnderstand.' Fear of shipwreck, piracy, and the innumerable perils of the sea must have given many anxious days and sleepless nights to some of the merchants of Bristol in the later sixteenth century. In an age of relatively slow communications it was essential that the merchant should know as quickly as possible any information that might affect the running of his business.

We may take it that the young merchant received plenty of good advice from his master before he sailed and that he probably carried with him a detailed briefing of the kind set out in *The Marchants Avizo* in the form of a 'Particular Remembrance.' He was expected to carry out precisely the instructions he had received from his master and from others for whom he was acting. If he had been told to purchase certain commodities, he must not ignore his orders and buy something else merely because it appeared to be cheap. He was given some elementary instruction in the laws of supply and demand and informed that 'ordinarily it falleth out, that the quantities of the best cheape wares that is brought home, hath smaller vtterance and lesse profite, than such deare wares as there commeth but verie little quantitie of.'

The Marchants Avizo urged the young apprentice always to seek advice from more experienced merchants on technical problems concerning currency, landing of wares, bills of exchange, and the prices at which he ought to buy and sell goods. There were in fact a number of Bristol merchants resident in Portugal and Spain, and one may assume that some of them would be willing to lend a helping hand to a beginner, at any rate as far as business routine was concerned.

But although he must obey explicit instructions and must seek advice from those more experienced than himself, the young merchant was expected to use his initiative and common sense. Overseas trade was an art, not a science, and the young man would have to make decisions on matters concerning which he had no precise orders. When he was making a sale, he was told 'lightly doe not refuse the second or third chapmans offer: for most ordinarily it falleth out, that the first and fourth offer is neuer so good as the third offer: but in this you are to haue a good insight your selfe, and to do according as is your hast and necessitie for your sales.'

One of the most important parts of the merchant's art consisted in making correct judgments on the qualities of the wines, spices, cloth, and other commodities offered for sale. A wrong judgment might mean a disastrous loss for the master, and this part of his work must have placed a severe strain on a young man who was probably taking full responsibility for the first time. Correct judgment depended so much on experience and on a flair for these things. No doubt the apprentice would have acquired some knowledge in his master's warehouse at home, but the author of *The Marchants Avizo* assisted him as far as he could by giving him a number of rule-of-thumb methods which would help him to reach a decision.

Accounting necessarily formed an important part of the merchant's work. Here again the young man would no doubt have already been instructed by his master, and he might possibly be acquainted with some of the early printed books on accounting which were beginning to appear in England in the second half of the sixteenth century; but John Browne nevertheless thought it desirable to provide his readers with a number of models suitable for the kind of work they would be undertaking. These accounts are straightforward records of sales and purchases, with details of the expenses involved in the various transactions. The apprentice was shown a simple method of calculating his commission of 2½ per cent, and was told how to convert Portuguese into Spanish currency. The accounts of a number of separate transactions involving both sales and purchases are finally summarized in an Account Current, which has cross-references to the folios which give the details of the transactions. There is nothing at all complicated about these accounts, although in their form and lay-out they are more advanced from the point of view of accountancy than those kept by Gresham's factor, Thomas Kitson, earlier in the century. They were no doubt intended to show the young man how to keep a methodical record of all his transactions abroad and to provide the merchant with the information he would need when making up his own books. The details given in them would also help to remind the beginner of some of the processes involved in overseas trade.

Another interesting feature of these accounts is that they seem to be based on the assumption that the trade would be conducted on a cash basis. The factor was not told how to record credit transactions. It may be that John Browne did not want to make things unduly complicated for the beginner, but it is also possible that credit played a smaller part in the Spanish and Portuguese trades than it did, for example, in the Netherlands trade.

Another very interesting section of *The Marchants Avizo* provided the reader with examples of the business documents used at the time. These include an insurance policy on the *Gabriel*, taken out by Thomas Aldworth and underwritten by two Londoners and a Bristol merchant. There are two different forms of bills of exchange, the one a bill of exchange for Spain, the other a bill of exchange to be made in England. The first takes the form of a draft order and may be said to show the influence of Italian business methods; the other is in the form not of a draft order but of an acknowledgment of debt, and this is more characteristic of Northern Europe. The collection of formularies does not, however, include a charterparty, perhaps because the young merchant would not need to bother about such a document in the early stages of his career.

Apprenticeship was traditionally intended to give a great deal more than simply a business training. The Society of Merchant Adventurers of England, for instance, laid down an elaborate code governing the conduct of its young men, thus recognizing 'its responsibility towards youths released from the discipline of the home and exposed to the temptations of life in a foreign town.' It is not known whether the Spanish Company had similar regulations, but the author of *The Marchants Avizo* certainly took very seriously his responsibility for the religious and moral training of his readers. He laid considerable stress on the need for prayer and meditation, and the young man was told to spend at least half an hour a day in these exercises, no matter how pressing his business; and he was given various suggestions as to the form they might take. When his ship arrived safely, his first thought must be to thank God for preserving him. He must never omit grace before meals. Possibly the author felt the need to emphasize these things all the more because his apprentice was being sent to countries where the religion was different from his own and where the opportunities for public worship according to the form used in the Church of England would be absent altogether. It is true John Browne does not say this, for he was anxious that his book should not give offence abroad, but this thought must surely have been in his mind.

The Marchants Avizo had a good deal of advice to give the young man regarding his business morality and the conduct of his private life. He was to be 'lowly, curteous, and seruiceable vnto every person.' He was to be scrupulously honest. He was not to play at any kind of games, especially dice or cards, and he was not to wear fine and costly apparel. He was to keep his promises and live well within his income. He was told: 'Be not greedy nor in lust after that, which is both displeasant vnto God: hurtfull to thy body; and enemy to thy soule: and a shortner of thy life: which is: Wine, Wealth and Women.' He was urged not merely to refrain from evil but to do good — to help the widow, the fatherless, the stranger, the poor, and the oppressed.

Although John Browne chose to incorporate the Spanish word *avizo* in the title of his book, he rather surprisingly made no attempt to persuade his readers to learn Spanish or Portuguese.[1] There seems to be little information on the extent to which English merchants did take the trouble to learn the language of those with whom they dealt. In the next century, the executors of the Bristol merchant John Whitson noted that he had a number of books, 'some Latin, some English and one Spanish book,' and this may suggest that such things were not common in Bristol. Presumably the merchants who resided abroad for any length of time became acquainted with the language, but no doubt much business was done through interpreters. Perhaps John Browne felt that his readers had enough to learn without struggling with Spanish or Portuguese. Some of them found

[1] The only other Spanish word in the book, apart from the names of coins, weights and measures, and customs duties, is "cabo" (small parcel). See p. 47, below.

English difficult to cope with when it was a question of putting their news into writing!

The Marchants Avizo contains so much detailed instruction to the young merchant concerning business techniques and personal conduct that it is perhaps unreasonable for the modern reader to complain of the omission of a great deal of information that he would like to find there. There is no reference, for example, to the Spanish Company to which all merchants trading to Spain and Portugal had to belong. There is no indication as to whether the Company had any kind of organization abroad to which the young man might turn for help. There are no hints about living conditions in Spain and Portugal, lodgings, transport, or procedure in foreign courts. We look in vain for any detailed commentary on the young man's duties at sea and on arrival at a port, and we learn nothing of local and national regulations prevailing in Spanish and Portuguese towns. Possibly the author of *The Marchants Avizo* thought these things could be best learned from experience. His little textbook was after all only an introduction to the subject, and, even as it stood, it contained plenty of strong meat which the novice would take some time to digest.

LATER EDITIONS OF THE MARCHANTS AVIZO

In spite of the fact that it first appeared in 1589 when England was at war with Spain, the book must have proved very popular, for a second edition was called for in 1590 and a third in 1591. It would be tedious to comment on all the variations among these editions. The version of 1591 contained 70 pages, in addition to preliminaries, whereas that of 1589 had only 68 pages, but the difference was due to lay-out and not to the inclusion of additional material. One is left with the impression that the author or the printer made some small alterations and corrections when a new edition was called for, but in the main left his work unchanged.

With the appearance of the third edition, the demands of the market were apparently satisfied for the time being.

In 1604 England made peace with Spain and in the following years the trade began to revive. In 1607 John Norton evidently decided that there would once more be a demand for the work and accordingly issued what was really the fourth edition. The name John

Browne no longer appeared in the Dedication and was replaced by the initials 'J. B.' The date '1587' was added in the margin after the note to the first verse of the poem, and the word 'King' was substituted for 'Queen' in the concluding verse. There were a number of differences in type and in the ornamental scrolls with which the work was embellished, and there were a great many changes in spelling. Little effort, however, was made to bring the work up-to-date. The young merchant was still urged: 'Honour thy Prince, for *she* hath power over life and death.' The documents and accounts were still dated 1589, and there was no indication of the fact that Thomas Aldworth and John Browne were both dead.

In 1616 Norton's partner, John Bill, brought out yet another edition. Later, on 26 August 1632, the rights in the book were transferred to Mistress Joyce Norton and Master Whitaker in accordance with a deed executed by the executors of John Bill, and the last edition was printed for Richard Whitaker in 1640.

The spelling varies considerably in all these editions, and in none of them is it entirely consistent throughout. There are differences also in type and ornament and in the various merchants' marks. There are some minor variations in the dates of the accounts, probably as a result of printers' errors. In general, however, these differences do not amount to very much, apart from the dropping of the name of John Browne, which appears only in the first three editions. Except for the first edition, all are printed on the same size paper and contain the same number of pages. The contents and lay-out of each page correspond practically word for word in all of them, except for minor differences due to the use of different types. None of them is in any way an enlargement of the first.

The Marchants Avizo does not seem to have been reprinted after 1640. Perhaps the last edition did not prove as successful as was hoped, for by then the work was over fifty years old and had been re-issued without revision of any kind.

THE MARCHANTS AVIZO IN RELATION TO OUR KNOWLEDGE OF ELIZABETHAN TRADE AND ELIZABETHAN MERCHANTS

The Marchants Avizo was not primarily intended to give an account of the organization of Elizabethan trade, nor was it meant to describe in detail all the economic processes and business techniques involved when a merchant of Bristol despatched a consignment of goods to the Iberian peninsula and received in return miscellaneous imports from Spain and Portugal. Nevertheless it does incidentally provide a certain amount of information on the way the trade was conducted. The letters, the accounts, and the other business documents may or may not be a record of events that actually happened, but from them it is possible to piece together a more or less connected story of the main stages in a trading venture of this kind.

For this particular voyage, Thomas Aldworth had loaded on the *Joseph* a cargo of cloth, wax, and lead. In addition, he had other consignments of goods on the *Gabriel*, which was probably his own ship and on which he took out an insurance from two Londoners and a Bristol merchant. He had to pay a premium of 7 per cent, but in view of the many dangers involved he no doubt considered it worth doing so, although many of his contemporaries were less cautious and preferred to stand the risks themselves. Some of his goods were also in the *Unicorn*, and we may assume that on this occasion a number of ships sailed in company for protection. The *Gabriel*, the *Minion*, and the *Joseph* arrived together at Lisbon, and the *Pleasure* was also associated with the venture. The practice of distributing goods among a number of different ships sailing in convoy had, of course, long been familiar to merchants.

When the fleet was ready, Robert Aldworth went on board the *Joseph*, no doubt dutifully carrying a copy of the 'General Remembrance' as well as instructions for this voyage in the form of a 'Particular Remembrance.' From it he knew what goods he was responsible for, what they had cost his master, and the minimum prices at which he might sell them. He was told what to buy in Spain and Portugal, and he was given a number of other instructions as well. It is clear that he was acting as factor for at least one other merchant as well as for his master.

In due course he set sail from Kingroad. His first letter concerning the contrary winds which had forced his ship into Milford, and the fact that he did not reach Lisbon until sixteen days after his departure, serve to remind us of the difficulties of communication in an age of sail. Even when he did reach Portugal, there was some delay before he could get on with his main business. He mentions without comment that he had not landed his goods or sold anything 'for it is but 3. dayes since we arriued.'

Meanwhile he had not been wasting his time. He had presumably arranged lodgings and contacted other merchants, including his master's friend 'W. O.' mentioned in his instructions. He was able to inform Thomas Aldworth of the current prices for various kinds of English cloth, as well as for lead and wheat, and to report on the prices of commodities in Portugal which would interest his master — pepper, cloves, mace, nutmegs, cinnamon, calico, soap, salt, and brasil or logwood. Ten or eleven days later, he wrote home giving details of the prices at which he had sold some of his cloth, wax, and lead. The cloth was bought by Jacques Magomes, draper, and the wax by Bernard Priget, merchant. On some of the cloth, he had been forced to give rebates. His 'impliments' or purchases consisted of pepper, supplied by Michael Sebra, merchant, and cloves, mace, and cinnamon bought of Lewis Betron and Martin Ferbuc.

In Lisbon the young man acted as agent for another English merchant for whom he sold broadcloth and shipped home pepper and cloves in the *Minion*. Another service he performed for this other merchant was to collect a debt and transmit the money by bill of exchange to Seville. It is not stated whether he was paid for this. There were established commission agents and factors prepared to undertake such tasks, but no doubt English merchants in the peninsula were prepared from time to time to do favours for each other.

On 7 November, the young man announced his intention of moving on to St. Lucar. It was, of course, quite common for those engaged in the Iberian trade to go first to Portugal and then to proceed to Spain. He did not apparently arrive in St. Lucar until December. There he sold the remainder of the cloth and lead brought out from England, and sent home oil, cochineal, and sack. Each consignment carried an appropriate merchant's mark and was accompanied by a bill of lading duly signed by the ship's purser. In transacting all this business, Robert Aldworth no doubt consulted his master's friend 'I. T.' in St. Lucar and gave him the token which Thomas Aldworth had sent from England.

In St. Lucar the young factor found himself in need of money in order to complete all the transactions ordered by his master, including the taking up of 15 tons of freight in the *Unicorn* to which

Thomas Aldworth was already committed. This contingency had been provided for in the 'Particular Remembrance,' and he went to 'T. M.' from whom he borrowed 100 duckets. He agreed to repay at the rate of six and eight pence a ducket, and issued a bill of exchange payable within fifteen days after the arrival of the *Gabriel* at her port of discharge in England.

Robert Aldworth did not remain all the time in St. Lucar, for on 25 January he wrote from Seville to a friend in Portugal asking him to take the letter to a certain draper in Lisbon and to receive from him 100 ducats which he had written to him to pay. It seems that the young man may have received further instructions from home after he left Portugal, for his friend was requested to spend the money on pepper and to ship it home to his master with an explanatory letter. Perhaps Thomas Aldworth had found that his pepper was fetching a good price and wanted a further consignment.

While he was still in Seville, Robert Aldworth wrote to another friend requesting him to receive a cargo of lead from the *Gabriel* when she arrived at St. Lucar. He was to sell it and with the proceeds to ride to Jerez and buy eight butts of the best sack. This was to be despatched to England, and the balance of the money was to be sent with all speed to the writer at Seville.

The purpose of the visit to Seville appears from the accounts, for Francisco Bera, who bought lead, and Sebastian de Laga, gentleman, who sold oil, both came from there. Pedris Meris, draper, who bought bays, came from St. Lucar, and the butts of sack were purchased from Martin de Leso, citizen of Jerez.

The accounts printed in *The Marchants Avizo* provide a certain amount of information about the actual conduct of trade. They show the kind of charges involved in shipping merchandise at Portuguese and Spanish ports, they list a variety of customs duties, and they refer to such practices as the double bagging of pepper, the watering of the pipes used for carrying oil, the cooperage of barrels both before and after they had been taken on board, and the sale of the covers which were placed over bales of cloth to protect them in transit.

The value of *The Marchants Avizo* lies not only in the data it gives concerning the techniques of trade but in the fact that, taken as a whole, it presents a vivid "inside" story of the problems confronting a merchant in his daily business. It reflects some of the actualities of commerce between England and the peninsula. Here we see the Elizabethan merchant concerned, not with the larger issues of international politics or the terms of trade, but with the smaller, yet very important questions as to whether his agents could write satisfactory letters or distinguish good woad from bad; and in this lies some corrective of the tendency to consider international trade only in terms of blind economic forces. A detailed account such as this one, based as it is on personal experience, adds a note of realism to the broad generalizations concerning the nature and extent of Elizabethan commerce; and it is all the more important because it is so rare.

Apart from what it has to say about the details of procedure and the techniques of commerce, *The Marchants Avizo* is also of interest because of what it tells us of the attitude of a merchant towards his profession. It cannot necessarily be assumed that John Browne was typical of his class, but his views are all the more interesting since so few of his fellow merchants expressed their ideas in writing.

One of the characteristics of *The Marchants Avizo* is the way in which advice on business matters is mixed with religious and moral teaching. Here, it may be suggested, the writer was continuing, against a rather different religious background, the medieval tradition that economics should not be divorced from ethics. It has been suggested by Mr. Louis B. Wright that the book 'epitomises the bourgeois philosophy that virtue pays in things of this world' and that 'with such good advice the business man was prepared to prosper both in this world and in the next.' Opinions will differ on this matter, but it might equally well be argued that the author does not seem to be concerned with teaching a morality suitable for those who wanted to have the best of both worlds, that he took his religion seriously, and that he did not consider it primarily in the light of the material advantages which it might or might not produce, although it is possible, young men being what they are, he felt no harm in pointing out that right conduct might incidentally make the apprentice a better merchant as well as a better man.

A recent controversy has focussed attention on the rise of the gentry in sixteenth century England. Under Elizabeth I the merchant class had not yet reached that social eminence which it attained later, but its importance was increasing. The introductory poem shows that the writer regarded the merchant as the cornerstone of the whole economy, and the main purpose of *The Marchants Avizo* was to help in training young men who should be worthy members of a great profession.

It is interesting to note in *The Marchants Avizo* the complete absence of the aggressive and nationalist spirit so often associated with Elizabethan England. This may in some measure indicate the personal outlook of the writer, but it is possible that it was shared by many merchants. War with Spain might be welcomed by the court gallant, the soldier of fortune, the sea-dog and the staunch Protestant, but for the merchant it too often meant trade depression. It is curious to find a writer urging his countrymen to be lowly and courteous in their conduct towards Spaniards in the year after the Armada.

It has been said of the medieval merchants that 'men who in their own transactions showed the greatest daring and inventiveness became circumspect and orthodox in giving advice to others. They tuned down their passions, their virtues, and their skills to an ideal of golden mediocrity.'[1] This seems to be true in some measure of the Elizabethan merchant, if John Browne can be regarded as typical. The measured tones of his work reflect nothing of the spirit of adventure of Elizabethan England. There is no indication of the excitement, the risks, and the worries necessarily involved in the perilous business of foreign trade, where fortunes made with difficulty could be so easily lost and where disaster might come suddenly upon the merchant through no fault of his own. Perhaps John Browne was content to go calmly on his way practising the virtues he preached and not worrying unduly about the risks of his calling. Perhaps he thought it best to teach his pupils the conventional rules of the game and to leave them to find out by experience the possibilities of playing it in less orthodox ways.

THE PLACE OF THE MARCHANTS AVIZO IN THE LITERATURE OF BUSINESS EDUCATION

In a recent collection of documents relating to medieval trade, Professors Lopez and Raymond provide a very interesting selection of medieval writings on commercial techniques and business practice. Not only were there treatises on arithmetic, accounting, geography

[1] Robert S. Lopez and Irving W. Raymond, Medieval Trade in the Mediterranean World, 1955, p. 408.

and trade routes, but there were manuals on general commercial practice which covered 'nearly every subject of interest to a merchant — descriptions of wares, measures, moneys, tariffs, itineraries, and sometimes complete *portolani*; arithmetic formulae to calculate compound interest; perpetual calendars; methods to make alloys and to test chemicals; economic theories, and advice on how to dodge customs inspection.' Most of what John Browne did in relation to certain branches of sixteenth century English trade had been done earlier in a different context, although neither he nor his contemporaries were aware of it. John Browne would have been surprised and no doubt pleased if he had known that the precursors of *The Marchants Avizo* included such works as *The Book of Knowledge of the Beauties of Commerce and of Cognizances of Good and Bad Merchandise and of Falsification*, probably written in ninth century Damascus by Abdu al-Fadl Ja'far ibn 'Ali al-Dimishqui, and *La Pratica della mercatura* of Francisco Balduccio Pegolotti, written in Florence in the early fourteenth century.

The development of a literature in English on the training of a merchant was surprisingly late. In his interesting Introduction to *An Essay on the Proper Method of Forming a Man of Business: 1716*, Professor Arthur H. Cole noted some of the early works in English on arithmetic, book-keeping, commercial law, and business morality which were 'more or less specifically designed for the education of the young or inexperienced merchant.' The number of such works was growing in the second half of the sixteenth century, but *The Marchants Avizo* appears to be the first general textbook of its kind printed in England. Mr. Louis B. Wright describes it as 'one of the best of these mercantile manuals of general information' and adds that 'no succeeding handbook managed to crowd so much useful and moral information into as brief a compass.'

The only other piece of Elizabethan economic writing that seems in any way comparable with *The Marchants Avizo* is a manuscript found among the State Papers, headed 'A speciall direction for divers trades of merchaundize to be used for soundrie placis upon adverticementes, as well for the chusinge of the time and wares for every of those placis. Most Beneficiall for those that use the trade of marchandize.' Unlike *The Marchants Avizo*, this work commented on the whole range of overseas markets with which Englishmen were concerned, but Spain and Portugal and their dependencies in fact received particular attention, and the German, Flemish and other markets were treated fairly briefly. Like the author of *The Marchants Avizo*, the writer was concerned to give practical advice on the conduct of trade. He supplied details of the different commodities to be found in the regions with which he was concerned and of the goods which could be most profitably exported to them. He gave information about prices and about the most suitable times of year for trading in particular markets. His work was full of hints about customs duties, safe-conducts, and other information necessary for a merchant. *A Speciall Direction* is reminiscent of *The Marchants Avizo* in its insistence on the importance of the trader's receiving accurate information on the state of the market: 'Item, take this for a generall Rule in all kinds of marchaundize, that yt is not Sufficient for yow to knowe all this, unless you Allwayes doe procuer to have adverticementes owt of all places; otherwyse you may be prevented by other men either before or After . . . Therefore adverticement is good and the principall thinge that belongeth to A Merchaunte.' We are again reminded of *The Marchants Avizo* in the passage which runs: 'And because that weight and mesure doth differ in many realmes, and in manye places of one realme, the first thinge that a marchante or factor dowth, after his cominge to any towne of trade, is to informe himesealfe of their weights and mesures, and so like wise of the cowstones and all other dewties . .'

A Speciall Direction has survived in a manuscript written in a clerkly hand which gives no clue to the authorship. It has been suggested on internal evidence that it was probably written by a west country merchant of broad practical experience in the decade 1575–85, and that it was intended for the perusal of some influential privy councillor whom in one place the author addressed as 'your honour.' Professor Conyers Read, who first printed the manuscript, thought that the endorsement might be in the hand of Sir Francis Walsingham, whose interest in trade is well known. It is tempting to suggest that there may be a connection between *The Marchants Avizo* and *A Speciall Direction*. Possibly John Browne was responsible for both, or possibly the link is to be found in Thomas Aldworth, who we know corresponded with Walsingham in 1582–83 in connection with Sir Humphrey Gilbert's proposed expedition.

If the material included in *A Speciall Direction* had been combined with that in *The Marchants Avizo*, the Elizabethan public would have had available an even more satisfactory manual on foreign commerce. *A Speciall Direction* was not in fact printed, but in an age when various 'Handbooks for Improvement' and 'Guides to Godliness' were appearing in increasing numbers to satisfy the demands of different sections of the community, the Elizabethan merchants could at least be grateful to the Bristolian who produced for them a first-rate textbook combining the two purposes of teaching young men business techniques and professional standards of behaviour. They showed their appreciation by demanding three editions in three years. The demand continued in the seventeenth century, for nothing quite so comprehensive appeared until Lewis Roberts published his *Merchants Map of Commerce* in 1638; and that was a folio volume of several hundred pages and very different from John Browne's little pocket instructor.

NOTES ON SOURCES

The great series of *Apprenticeship Books* and *Burgess Books* in the Bristol Record Office provide a number of details relating to the Brownes and the Aldworths. The *Mayor's Audits* record payments made during John Browne's mayoralty and contain a collection of his signatures as auditor. From the *Ordinances of Common Council* it is possible to trace some details of the part he played in the city government. A copy of his will is to be found in the *Great Orphan Book* (Register Book of Wills), vol. III, fo. 6ff. Also deposited in the Bristol Record Office are the parish registers of the church of St. Nicholas, Bristol, which record Browne's marriage and burial, as well as the christenings and burials of other members of his family.

A Speciall Direction etc., was printed by Conyers Read in the *English Historical Review*, xxix, 1914, pp. 515–24; by N. S. B. Gras in *The Evolution of the English Corn Market*, 1915, pp. 429–39; and by R. H. Tawney and Eileen Power in *Tudor Economic Documents*, 1924, III, pp. 199–210.

Some details concerning the registration of *The Marchants Avizo* can be found in *A Transcript of the Registers of the Company of Stationers of London, 1554–1640*, edited by Edward Arber, II, 249; IV, 249.

Adams's Chronicle of Bristol, which makes some reference to events in John Browne's mayoralty, was published in Bristol in 1910.

There are a number of references to the Bristol branch of the Spanish Company in *Records relating to the Society of Merchant Venturers of the City of Bristol in the Seventeenth Century*, edited by Patrick McGrath, Bristol, 1952.

Comments on *The Marchants Avizo* are to be found in Lt. Colonel Bramble, 'A Rare Bristol Book,' *Proceedings of the Clifton Antiquarian Club, 1888–1893*, Exeter, 1893, pp. 251–58; in Louis B. Wright, *Middle-Class Culture in Elizabethan England*, University of North Carolina Press, 1935, pp. 160–62; and Jean Robertson, *The Art of Letter Writing—An Essay on the Handbooks published in English during the sixteenth and seventeenth centuries*, University of Liverpool Press, 1942.

Professor Arthur H. Cole has some very interesting remarks to make on the development of business literature in his introduction to *An Essay on the Proper Method of Forming a Man of Business: 1716.* In a recently published collection of documents entitled *Medieval Trade in the Mediterranean World*, Professors Robert S. Lopez and Irving W. Raymond include a section dealing with Manuals, Accounting Methods, Commercial Correspondence, and Moral Standards and Practical Advice, which provide interesting comparisons with the material to be found in *The Marchants Avizo.* Gordon Connell-Smith's *Forerunners of Drake; A study of English Trade with Spain in the early Tudor Period*, London, 1954, contains a good deal of material relating to the techniques of the Anglo-Spanish trade.

A NOTE ON THE DIFFERENT EDITIONS AND THEIR LOCATIONS

A. *1589 edition.* The only known copy is in the Library of St. John's College, Oxford, bound up with nine other pamphlets printed between 1593 and 1681. The title page is reproduced as a frontispiece in the present edition and its text is followed. There is a microfilm copy in the Kress Library, Graduate School of Business Administration, Harvard University.

The publisher, William Norton (1527–1593), was a son of Andrew Norton of Bristol. He was one of the original freemen of the Stationers' Company of London and had a large number of books printed for him (see E. Gordon Duff, *A Century of the English Book Trade*, London, Bibliographical Society, 1905, p. 112, and the *Dictionary of National Biography*).

The printer, Richard Field, was a son of Henry Field, tanner, of Stratford-on-Avon. After an apprenticeship to Thomas Vautrollier, he took up the freedom of the Stationers' Company on 4 March 1587. *The Marchants Avizo* was one of the earliest books printed by him. His principal device was the "Anchora Spei" which he took over from Vautrollier (see *A Dictionary of Printers and Booksellers in England, Scotland and Ireland*, London, Bibliographical Society, 1910, pp. 102–3).

Ecclesiasticus 40.18, quoted in part on the title page of the first edition, reads: "To labour and to be content with that a man hath, is a sweete pleasant life: and that is, to find treasure of all treasures." (*The Holy Bible*, printed at London by Christopher Barker, 1584.) John Browne may have felt on reflection that the sentiment was not entirely suitable for budding merchants whose aim was presumably to increase their wealth. A different quotation was used in later editions.

B. *1590 edition.* The only known copy is in the possession of Mr. P. E. Tyhurst of Gatcombe Park, Minchinhampton, Stroud, Gloucestershire. The title page reads: "THE/MARCHANTS/AVIZO./ VERIE NECESSARIE FOR/their Sonnes and seruants, when they/first send them beyond the Seas, as to/*Spayne and Portingale or other/Countreyes.*/Made by their hartie wellwiller in Christ./I. B. Marchant./ Eccles. 1.Chap. 11.verse./ The feare of the Lord is glorie, and gladnes and reioycing, and a/ ioyfull crowne, &c./ Imprinted at London by Thomas Orwin, by/ the assignes of William Norton./ 1590." There appears on the title page a printer's device of two clasped hands holding a caduceus and two cornucopias, encircled by the words: "By Peace Plenty. By Wisdom Peace." (see Ronald B.

McKerrow, *Printers and Publishers in England and Scotland*, London, Bibliographical Society, 1913, pp. 105–6, illustrations nos. 273 and 374).

The copy is unbound and consists of pages sewn together, presumably as originally issued by the printer, but a number of pages at the end of the work are missing. It consists of 8 pages of preliminaries (title page, dedication, poem, and contents list) followed by 62 numbered pages. The 1589 edition has 68 numbered pages and the 1591 edition has 70 numbered pages. It is probable that the 1590 edition also contained 70 numbered pages, for its general layout is closer to the 1591 edition than to the 1589 edition, and the editions of 1590 and 1591 were both printed by Thomas Orwin.

The 1590 edition is not a reprint of the edition of 1589. Someone, probably the author, took the opportunity of making a number of small alterations in the text, some of which are pointed out in the notes of this edition, and there are some variations in the merchants' marks used in the margin.

C. *1591 edition.* Two copies are known. One is in the Huntington Library, California; the other, in the New York Public Library. The title page is the same as in the edition of 1590, except for the date.

This edition contains the usual preliminaries followed by pages numbered from 1 to 70. It is very like that of 1590, but there are a number of minor variations which show that it was not simply a reprint.

D. *1607 edition.* There are seven known copies of this edition. Copies are to be found in the British Museum; the National Maritime Museum, Greenwich; the Goldsmiths' Library, University of London (2 copies); the Bodleian Library; and the Chapin Library, Williams College, Williamstown. Another is in the possession of Messrs. Page & Co., Solicitors, 2, Bristol Chambers, Bristol 1. The title page reads: "THE/MERCHANTS/AVIZO./ VERIE NECESSARIE FOR/ their Sons and Seruants, when they/first send them beyond the Seas, as to/*Spaine and Portingale, or other Countries./Made by their heartie welwiller in Christ,*/I. B. Merchant./*Eccles. 1. Chap. 11 verse.*/ The feare of the Lord is glorie, and gladnes, and reioycing, and/a ioyfull crowne, &c/LONDON/Imprinted by John Norton./1607."

The printer's device on the title page is the clasped hands and cornucopias as in the editions of 1590 and 1591.

The main difference between this edition and earlier ones is that the name of John Browne no longer appears in the dedication, and the words "From my house in Bristow the 26 day of October, 1589" are omitted. Apart from this, the edition is essentially the same as those of 1590 and 1591, but there are considerable variations in spelling.

One of the two copies in the Goldsmiths' Library, University of

London, is bound up with a number of other seventeenth century pamphlets. The title page is missing and a facsimile reproduction has been inserted. The original title page is presumably the one in the Bagford Collection in the British Museum (Harley 5949 No. 167 fo. 65 v).

Messrs. Page's copy is the one formerly in the possession of Lt. Colonel Bramble and described by him in *The Proceedings of the Clifton Antiquarian Club*, November, 1892. The copy in the National Maritime Museum came from the collection at Lowther Castle, Penrith, owned by the Earl of Lonsdale.

E. *1616 edition.* Copies are known to exist in the British Museum; the Bodleian Library, Christ Church, Oxford; the Library of Congress; the Kress Library, Harvard Graduate School of Business Administration; the Central Reference Library, Bristol; and the Massachusetts Historical Society.

The title page reads: "THE/MERCHANTS/AVIZO./ VERY NECESSARY FOR/their Sonnes and Seruants, when they/first send them beyond the Sea, as to/ *Spaine and Portingale, or other*/Countries./ *Made by their hearty welwiller in Christ,*/ I. B. *Merchant*/. *Eccles.* 1. *Chap.* 11 *verse.* The feare of the Lord is glory, and gladnesse, and reioycing,/and a ioyfull crowne, &c./. LONDON, Printed by JOHN BILL./1616."

The printer's device is a winged mercury standing with one foot on a globe (see Ronald B. McKerrow, *Printers and Publishers Devices*, p. 352 and No. 382).

Substantially this edition is the same as that of 1607, but there are numerous variations in spelling, and the printer used merchants' marks different from those utilized earlier.

F. *1640 edition.* Copies are to be found in the British Museum; the Bodleian Library; the National Library of Scotland; Queen's College, Oxford; the Folger Library; New York Public Library; and Columbia University Library.

The title page reads: "THE / MARCHANTS / AVIZO, / OR / Instructions very necessary for / their Sonnes and Servants, when / they first send them beyond the Sea, as to / *Spaine*, and *Portingale*, or other / Countries./ Written by a wel-willer to youth, I. B. / Merchant in *Bristoll.* / London, / Printed by E. G. for *Richard Whitaker*, and are to / be sold at his shop at the signe of the Kings Armes / in Saint *Pauls* Churchyard, 1640."

The printer's device consists of three feathers.

This edition is substantially the same as those of 1607 and 1616 and, like them, contains the usual preliminaries followed by 70 numbered pages, but again there are numerous variations in spelling and some differences in the merchants' marks.

ACKNOWLEDGEMENTS

I wish to express my thanks to the President and Fellows of St. John's College, Oxford, for permission to reproduce the title page and to print the text of the edition of 1589, and to Mr. H. M. Colvin, Librarian of St. John's College, for the assistance he has given me in my task.

Professor William A. Jackson of Harvard has very kindly helped me to locate the various surviving copies of *The Marchants Avizo*, and a number of librarians and private owners have allowed me to examine their copies or have given me information concerning them. Mr. P. E. Tyhurst generously deposited in the University of Bristol Library the only known copy of the 1590 edition so that I might examine it at my leisure.

I am deeply grateful to Professor Arthur H. Cole, Librarian of the Harvard University Graduate School of Business Administration, for his many valuable suggestions and criticisms, and for all the trouble he has taken in preparing this work for the press.

My colleagues, Mr. Peter Ramsey and Mr. Baril Cottle, gave me the benefit of their specialist knowledge on a number of problems.

Professor T. C. Mendenhall and Professor T. S. Ashton made some very helpful suggestions concerning the publication of the work, and Mr. C. E. Pitman very kindly helped me in the arrangements for an English edition.

I must express my gratitude to the Colston Research Society of the University of Bristol for making a grant towards the cost of publication.

PATRICK MCGRATH
UNIVERSITY OF BRISTOL

THE MARCHANTS AVIZO

VERY NECESSARIE FOR THEIR

sonnes and seruants, when they first send them beyond the seas, as to Spaine and Portingale or other countreyes.

Made by their hartie wellwiller in Christ. I.B. Marchant.

ECCLES. 40.18.

To labour and to be content with that a man hath, is a sweet life: but the feare of God is aboue all, &c.

Imprinted at London by Richard Field for William Norton, dwelling in Paules Churchyard at the signe of the Queenes armes.
1589.

CONSTANTINI CRVX.

TO THE WORSHIPFVL
MAISTER THOMAS ALDWORTH

Marchant of the citie of Bristowe:[1] and to all the worshipfull companie of the Marchants of the said citie:[2] your bounden in good will Iohn Browne, wisheth vnto your worships, felicitie in heauen, and prosperitie in earth.

WOrshipfull, upon verie earnest motion & persuasion of a friend unto me, to set foorth in publick this matter, which I onely had made priuate for instruction of me and mine. And then calling to remembrance some necessitie and dutie: necessitie, because by mine own experience I know how greatly my selfe and many other my countrimen, at our first going into Spaine were troubled with difficulties, for want of such a patterne as this, for ease of our tender wittes. And dutie, because I acknowledge myself bounde̅,[3] both to your Worship, and to all those of my profession, to employ my whole labours to do you any pleasure or profit that I might. I therefore haue emboldened myselfe to dedicate and offer this my poore myte unto [y]our Worships: wherby not onely your name may therin be still remembred, but may also make manifest your kind fauours, who are still willing to be furtherers of any generall good. Mine owne labour or skill I confesse, is but very litle or nothing in this thing, because I myselfe do but only as a poore willing labourer, to help forwards that worke, the foundation & platforme wherof, is setled and builded alreadie. But my chiefe purpose herein is, onely to worke a generall ease to all Marchants: whereby they may the lesse trouble themselues, either with writing, inuention, or thought of these matters. And like wise that it might be some stay to young and weake wits: yeelding them therby the more freedome of mind toward their other businesse. Being carefull in myselfe to order this worke, that not onely (as I hope) it shalbe lawfully permitted to be seene and read in anie parts beyond the *sea[4]: but also shal instruct yong nouices, to vse greater breuitie in their writings then commonly they are wont.

** If this booke may not be thought tollerable beyond the seas: then will it be yet a good exercise and but little labour, for euery prentice to copie it all out in writing: and so carie it with him for his instruction.*

Wherefore I commit my selfe and my doings, first to the praise of God, and then to your good acceptance and fauourable patronage. Desiring your Worships all, that howsoeuer you do determine of the unabilitie of this my labour: yet that you vouchsafe to take in good part the abilitie of my loue and good meaning in it. So I rest, beseeching God to giue unto you all, eternall felicitie in heauen, and prosperitie to your liues end here on earth.

From my house in Bristow the 26. day of October. 1589.

Your Worships bounden
in good will.

I. B.[5] MAR.

To the Reader

When marchants trade proceedes in peace.
And labours prosper well:
Then common weales in wealth increase,
As now good *proofe can tell

** This was spoken when was a long staye of the marchdntes [sic] trade, to the great decay of many a one.*[6]

For when the marchants trade was free,
His ventures for to make:
Then euery art in his degree
Some gaines thereof did take.

The marchant made the Clothier rich
By venting of his cloth:[7]
The Clothier then sets many at worke,
And helpeth euery crafte.

For first the Spinster [8] hereby liue,
The Weauer and the Dier:
By cloth, the Shearman also thriue,
When Marchant is the buyer.

The Landlord and the Tenant sell,
By this meanes all their wooll:
Their Biefe, their Corne, they sell the more,
When Marchants purse grow full.

The Grocer with the Vintener,
The Mercer profit reape:
When Spices, Silks, and Wines, come store,
By Marchants ventures great.

The Vitler and the Husbandman,
And handicraftes ech on:
Make gaines when Merchāts Ships & goods
Doe merily come home.

The Sailers herehence gets their skill,
To rule the stately Ship,
And so become right worthy men,
For Sea and Land most fit.

Yea diuers more the Marchants trade,
Doth succour and relieue:
As Bargeman, Craneman, Porter eke,
To him that Cart doth driue.

Let no man then grudg Marchants state,
Nor wishe him any ill:
But pray to God our Queene to saue,
And Marchants state help still.

I B

THE TABLE OF THOSE THINGS

which are contained in this Booke.

A GENERALL REMEMBRANCE
FOR A SERVANT WHEN HE FIRST

trauelleth to the Sea, as to Spaine or Portingale, or other countreyes.

Emanuel[9]

A General remembrance for you my seruant I. A.[10] that when it pleaseth God you shall trauell vnto the sea, first & principally you doe not forget vpon your safe arriuall at your Port, to giue vnto God most hartie and *humble thankes for his gracious protection of you, by saying as in token of your thankefulnesse, some godly prayer of thankesgiuing, or say onely with reuerence the Lords Prayer, giuing him withall thankes in some wordes of your owne spirit.[11]

** For to feare God and to bee thankefull vnto him, is the beginning of all happinesse and prosperitie in our affaires.*

Secondly, that presently vpon your ariuall, you doe make diligent inquirie,[12] whether anie ships be bound either to this Port of Bristowe, or to any part of England. And then haue especiall care, that the neerest that commeth to this Port, you write letters by them vnto me, and to them that you haue to deale for, of the arriuall of your ship: according to this plaine and briefe forme of inditing, as I will hereafter shew you. And so write likewise by your first letters, of the state of your businesse, and of the newes of the country, according as that time passeth. And when you haue learned of anie ship that commeth for England, doe not yourselfe make it *knowne to anie bodie at all: but write and deliuer your letters secretlie, for it shall sound much to your especiall credit and good liking, when your diligence shall be so seene, that your letters shall shew the first arriuall of your Ship: because it is the thing that euerie Marchant doth especially long after to vnderstand.[14]

** This I say: to procure the more care and diligence in a youth.*[13]

Thirdly, deale closely & secretly in all your affaires and busynes, and before you enterprise any thing, doe you after curteous and gentle manner aske counsel, either of some Marchant in the Ship, or your Hoste, or of some Englishman: how you are to deale about your wares, both touching the landing it, the customing it, the selling it, the receauing of your moneyes, the buying of any wares againe, the customing the same againe, and to haue out all your writs and dispatches for euery such thing, as is needfull to be had. And hauing bin thus once instructed, do you with carefullnes remember it of yourselfe against another time. Also be earnest in noting & marking euery thing that you may, but be yourselfe as secret and silent as is possible.

Fourthly in any case shew yourselfe lowly, curteous, and seruiceable vnto every person: for though you & many of vs else may think, that too much lowlinesse bringeth contempt and disgrace vnto vs: yet assuredly (it is wel known by experience) that there springeth of no one vertue so great fruit vnto vs, as of gentlenesse and humilitie: for it will both appease the anger and ill will of our enemies, & encrease the good will of our friends.[15] Also in any wise be not seduced by any person, to play at any kinde of game, especially dice or cards, nor to vse feasting or banketing, or keeping company with women, nor to go fine and costly in apparell: for all these things are especially noted, and doe bring any yong beginner to vtter discredit and vndoing.

Fiftly carie this for an especiall note, that whensoeuer you haue dealings for anie marchants, you do in all things and euerie point obserue according to their commission and direction. For although I knowe, it wil sometimes seeme to your selfe, that you shall better please your marchant, not to buy those wares which he appointeth, because of the dearenesse of them: yet (I say) you shall giue euermore best contentment to your marchant, and saue your selfe harmelesse, when you followe his owne order and remembrance. And take this also for a caueat, that you neuer think the same ware which is best cheape, and is most bought vp, that it will be best to bestow your money theron: for ordinarily it falleth out, that the quantitie of the best cheape wares that is brought home, hath smaller vtterance and lesse profite, than such deare wares as there commeth but verie litle quantitie of. Also be carefull in setting vp safely your money when you haue receaued it: and likewise be warie whē you receiue your moneys for your wares, crauing the paines of some marchant your freind, as to helpe you the first time to receaue it for you, vntill you haue more knowledge to receaue it yourselfe.

Moreouer be you in any wise circumspect touching your behauior when you be in the countrey of Spaine or elsewhere: and shewe yourselfe lowly and courteous to all people, and learne what be their ciuill lawes and customes, and be carefull to keepe them. If anie of the rude and common sort of people (as so it is in all countreys) will by chaunce offer you anie abuse or wrong, appease them againe rather by sufferance and gentlenesse, then by reuenge: for so shall you best quiet your selfe, & ouercome your enemie. In the sales of your wares, doe you, before you set price of it to any man, make inquirie howe other Englishmen haue sold the like commodities, and so do you accordingly set price of yours. And lightly doe not refuse the second or third chapmans offer: for most ordinarily it falleth out, that the first and fourth offer is neuer so good as the third offer: but in this you are to haue a good insight your selfe, and to do according as is your hast and necessitie for your sales.

Be most faithful & iust in al your accompts with euery man, & defraud no man willingly not the value of a farthing. See that at no time you do take any mans doings or dealings into your hands, without my leaue and counsell: because by the trouble of other mens businesse, you may neglect & frustrate mine owne. And haue also regarde, for those small aduentures which I shall licence you to make for your owne priuate benefit, that euery voiage you doe deliuer me an accompt of it, wherby from time to time I may see and know your estate, and what of right doeth aperteine vnto you. Be circumspect and nigh in all your expences; making your reckoning, that what you now spare and saue vnto me, it may grow the more to your owne benefit in time to come.

Lastely, let this be yet your first and chiefest point in all your actions:[16] that especially you omit not your dutifull seruice towards almighty God, but euerie morning and night, to pray that God will still prosper and protect you, & to giue him humble thankes that he hitherto hath alwayes mercifully defended you. And this doe you performe, by saying silentlie, reuerently, & atentiuely, such praiers as you haue learned by hart: or if your memorie cannot well remēber any other praier, say only to the praise of the blessed Trinity, the *Lords praier and the *Creed, vsing euermore withall these three pointes of meditation. First, to meditate your sinnes and aske God hartely mercy, and stedfastly purpose amendment. Secondly, meditate Gods benefits: and humbly thanke him. Thirdly, meditate your necessities: and craue his holy helpe for them. The which you may

** This order of prayer I have thought, might be good and godly: both because of the country beyond the seas, and because of marchants lets and hinderance to continue in long prayer.*

then conclude the effect of these meditations, by saying lastly againe the Lords praier. And this dutiful exercise of praier, I do require you neuer once to pretermit both at morning & at night, how hastie and vrgent soeuer be your businesse. For how great equitie & reason is it, that we should spend at the leaste one halfe houre or litle moment of the day in thanks, seruice, and mindfullnes of God: who is both carefull & mindfull to serue & succour vs, euen all the whole day and euer all our life long. Also neuer sit downe, or rise vp from meate, but be mindfull of God: & in expressing your thanksgiuing, say some Godly grace or other: or only say (rather then faile) no more then, *In the name of the father, of the sonne, & of the Holy Ghost*, & let those wordes shew your thankfulnes to God. Finally in all your actions, vse diligence, conscience, silence and patience. Thus making no doubte, but if you be mindfull of your dutie and seruice to God, all thinges shall go well and haue happy successe that you take in hand. But contrarie doing: your labours will not prosper, nor anie thing that you doe, will euer come to good passe or perfection. The holy Ghost be euermore your Protector.

Yours master doe you any good that
you shall deserue.

T. A.

HERE FOLLOWETH A BRIEFE FORME OF ALL SUCH LETTERS AS YOU SHALL NEEDE TO WRITE THROUGHOUT YOUR WHOLE VOYAGE.

The which forme is effectual & sufficient inough, and may still be obserued, vntill by experience you may learne to indite better you selfe.

A Letter written to your Master, if your ship be forced by weather into any place, before you come to your Port of discharge.

Emanuel

After my dutie remembred, I pray for your good health and prosperity &c. These are certifying you, that by meanes of ill weather and contrarie winds, we were withing vi. dayes after our departure from Kingrode,[17] forced into Milford: where here we abide according to Gods pleasure, hoping that he will shortly better prouide for vs. Little newes I heare worth the writing: onely I vnderstand that there is (*Here write your newes if you haue anie.*) Thus taking my leaue with my dutifull commendations to my good mistresse &c.[18] I heartely desire of God to protect and prosper you and all yours. From Milford the 4. day of October 1589.

Your faithful and obedient
seruant

R.A.[19]

A Letter to be written to your Master presently upon arriuall at your Port.

Emanuel.

After my duetie remembred, I pray for your good health & prosperitie, &c. These are certifying you, that on the 24. day of October, withing 16. dayes after our departure from Kingrode, we arriued here at Lisbon (God be thanked) in good safetie, and the Gabriel and the Minnyon also.[20] As yet we haue not landed our goods nor sold anie thing, for it is but 3. dayes since we arriued. Touching Sales or Impliments,[21] I doe vnderstand that it wil not fall out so well as I wished or hoped it would: but I will do my verie best indeuour for you according as time serue.

Brode clothes of the finest sorts, I do heare may be worth about 50. Duckets: and sorting clothes 38. Duckets: fine Stammels 80. Duckets a cloth: Reading Kerseis about 14. Duckets a peece: Bayes about 12. Duckets a peece:[22] Lead 19. Rials the Kintall: wheat 3 Rials and a halfe the Alquer. Of the wares here of the countrey: pepper is worth about 50. Duckets the Kintal: cloues 75. Duckets: maces 80. Dks: Nutmegs 80. Duckets: Sinamond 68. Duckets:

Callicowes of Sancto Passes[23] at 50. Duckets the Corge: Sope at 7. Duckets the Kintal: Brasill at 7. Duckets and a halfe the Kintall: Oyles 86. Duckets the tunne: Salt at 11 Rials the Muy[24] *Litle newes I heare worth the writing, onely it is sayd that the king, &c. (*Here write your newes.*) Thus taking my leaue, with my dutifull commendations remembred to my good Mistresse, &c.[26] I heartely desire of God to protect and prosper you and all yours. From Lisbon the 27. day of October 1589.

** Note that you inquire & also write the pryses of all other vendible warrs*[25]

Your faithful seruant
whiles I liue,
R.A.[27]

A Letter to be written to your Maister, or some other man that is of worship, next after your first letter.

Emanuel

AFTER my duetie remembred vnto your Worship: I pray your good health & prosperitie, &c. These are certifying your worship, that by a ship of London called the Marchant royall, I wrote to you before of our arriuall here at Lisbon. But lest some chance should let the comming of it to your hands, you shall againe vnderstand that on the 24. day of October, within 16. dayes after our departure from Kingrode, we arriued here at Lisbon (God be thanked) in good safetie, and the Minion and the Gabriel also. Touching Sales or Implimēts it falleth not out so well as I hoped and wished it would: but I haue done my very best indeuor for you as time serued. Your 10. fine brode clothes, I sold them for 50. Duckets and 6. rials a peece: but they forced me in rebates 8 Duckets vpon thē all.[28] Your Stammell brode cloth I haue sold for 84. Duckets and 3. Rials. Your lead I haue sold for 23. Rials the Kintall. The waxe for 24. Duckets and a halfe the Kintall. As for your impliments, I haue according vnto your remembrance laden for you in the Gabriell, 6. Kintals and 2. Roues of pepper, which cost the first pennie 50. Duckets the Kintall.[29] Also in that ship 1. Kintall of

Cloues which cost the first pennie 75. Duckets and a halfe: and haue marked it all according to your marke in the margent.[30]

Mases are here worth 80. Dkts. the Kintall: Sinamond 68. Dks. Nutmegs 80. Dks. Callicowes of S. Passes at 50. Dks. the Corge. Oyles 86. Duckets the tun: sope at 7. Dks. the kintall: brasil 7. Dks & a half the kintal: salt 11. rials the Muy. Of our English commodities: Reding kersies are worth 14. Dks. a peece: bayes 9 Dks. 4 rials a peece: wheat 3. rials & a halfe the Alquer, &c.

Within this fower dayes we hope to make readie to go for Andalozia: God be our good speede whensoeuer we go. In Andalozia we vnderstād that oyles are worth about 78. Duckets the tunne: and Secks 12. Duckets the But. Little newes I heare worth the writing: &c. Thus taking my leaue, I commit your worship to Almightie God. From Lisbon the 7. day of Nouember. 1589.

Your Worships at commandement
to the vttermost of my power,
R.A.

A Letter to be written upon your arriuall from Lisbon vnto your second Port

Emanuel

After my duetie remembred, I pray for your good health & prosperitie, &c. These are certifying you, that on the 7. day of December, within 5. dayes after our departure from Lisbon, we arriued at S. Lucar (God be thanked) in good safetie. Touching sales or impliments here, it falleth out not so well as I hoped and wished it would; but I haue done my very best indeuour for you as the time serued. Your 12. peeces of bayes I haue sold for 11. Ds. and 7. Rials the peece: and your 15. tunnes of lead, after 21 Rials the Kintal, &c. (*Here write forwards as it is in the Letter next before, chāging onely the names of the wares which you haue to buy or sell in that countrey.*)

Your faithfull and obedient
seruant, R.A.

A Letter to be sent in that ship where you haue laden goods for any Marchant

Emanuel

** Note that whē you write to a Marchant or any other which is not your Maister or is not a man of worship: then may you well inough begin alwayes your letters after this maner.*

AFTER* my very heartie commendations vnto you, I pray for your good health and prosperitie, &c. These are certifying you, that I haue laden for your accompt in the Gabriell of Bristow according to your remembrance, 4. tuns of oyle, which is marked with your mark in the margent. The which dost cost the first pennie 11. Rials and a halfe the Roue, and doth amount unto 75. Duckets, 3 Rials the tunne. More I haue laden for you 2. Roues of Cochenele, which cost after 160 Duckets the Kintal, and is marked according to the other marke. More 12. buts of Seck which cost the first peny 15. Ds. the But: marked also with the former. Al which goods (God willing) I hope you shal well and safely receaue. Here within inclosed I send you a bill of lading for all your goods and likewise your accompt. Thus for this time I take my leave, trusting my selfe very shortly to be at home, for by the grace of God I purpose to come alongst in the *Pleasure*:[31] vntill which time I commit you to Almightie God. From S. Lucar the 23. day of december. 1589.

Your assured to my power.

R.A.

A Letter to be writen to one that hath left some busines to doe for him under your handes, there in the Country.

Emanuel

AFTER my verie hartie comendations vnto you, I pray for your good health and prosperitie, &c. These are certifying you, that touching such busines which you apointed me to do for you: I haue now sold the 4. brode clothes which you left here with me, for 48. Dks. a peece: and haue imploied the monie according to your direction. Namely in 1. Kintall of pepper, which cost the first penny 45. Duckets and a halfe the kintall, and haue laden it in the Minion. More in the same ship I haue laden 3. Roues of cloues, which cost after 76 duckets the kintall, and haue marked it all with your mark

as in the margent.[32] The mony which you appointed me to receaue of F.B. he hath paid it me: and I haue passed it (and all the rest of the monie in my hands, being in the whole 184. Duckets, 2 Rials): by exchange to Siuill in B.E.[33] as was your remembrance. I do send you your accompt here within enclosed. Also your letter that you left with me, I haue sent by my brother in law I.R. in the Tobie.[34] I pray you do my harty cōmendacions vnto my good frends at Bristow, master I.P. &c. Little newes I heare worth the writing. Thus taking my leaue I commit you to Almightie God. From Lisbon the 5. day of Ianuarie 1589.

Yours assured to my power,
R.A.

A Letter to be written to a friend, giuing him thanks for some pleasures he hath done for you, and requesting againe some farther good turne of him

Emanuel

After my very harty cōmendations vnto you, I pray for your good health & prosperitie, &c. These are giuing you most heartie thanks for your great pains & gentlenesse heretofore shewed vnto me: assuring you that you shall find me to the vttermost of my power, both gratefull and mindfull to pleasure you againe in the like & greater if I be able. Desiring you hartily yet once more, to let me craue so much your good wil, as to do me againe this one plesure: which is, to deliuer this letter hereinclosed to master P.R. Draper,[35] that dwelleth in Lisbon in *Roa noua*: and that you would receaue for me of him 100. Duckets which I haue written to him to pay you. And when you haue receaued it, that you would be so good as to imploie it all in good pepper, & to set my Masters mark on it, which is as in the margent.[36] Praying you to agree for freyte, and to procure to haue it laden in the *Pleasure*, & to write a letter vnto my Master about it. I am sory that I am driuen to make still so bold vpon you: wishing that you had the like or greater occasion to trye also my good will towards you. Little newes I heare worth the writing &c.

Thus taking my leaue, I commit you to Almightie God. From Ciuel 25 day of Ianuary. 1589.

Your assured to my power.
R.A.

A Letter to be written to a friend when you would haue him to pleasure you in any matter.

Emanuel

AFTER my very hartie comendations vnto you: I pray for your good health and prosperitie. &c. These are most hartely to desire so much your friendship and good will, to doe me this pleasure: as to receaue for me out of the Gabriel when she cometh to S. Lucar, 6. tũnes of Lead conteining 105. peeces, being marked as in the *margent: & to doe so much as make present sale of it, the best you can as the time serueth. And when you haue made sale and receaued monyes for it, that you would be so good as to ride vnto Sheres and buy for me 8. Buts of very good Secke the best that possible can be gotten, though they cost a Ducket or two the more in a But: & to lade them away as soone as is possible abord the Gabriel, marking them with the former marke in the margent.[37] And the rest of the monies that you shal haue left, I pray you to passe it with all speede hither to Siuil vnto me. Herein (if without seeming ouerbold) I may craue you pains to pleasure me: I doe assure you that you shall finde me to the vuttermost of my power, both gratefull and mindful to pleasure you againe in the like and much greater if I can be able. Little newes I heare worth the writing. Thus taking my leaue I commit you to Almightie God. From Siuil the 27. day of Ianuarie. 1589.

Yours assured to my power, R.A.

THIS BREEFE & PLAINE ORDER IN YOUR LETTERS, I THINKE IT BEST YOU SHOULD FOR A TIME VSE, BECAUSE OF EASING A WHILE YOUR OWNE YOUNG INUENTION OF INDITING: FOR

AFTER THIS MANER OF STILE YOU MAY WRITE TO MOST SORTES OF PERSONS.

The superscription of your letters may thus.

To the worshipfull, Alderman Aldworth Marchant,
dwelling in Smal streat in Bristow: giue this with speed.
Or saie: to the worshipfull my Master, Master Jhon Barker
marchant. &c.[38]
Or: to my assured good friend Master Thomas Pits
marchant. &c.[39]

CERTAINE ESPECIALL BRIEF NOTES OF WAIGHTS,

measures and value of monies in Portingale, Spaine and France, with an instruction for the better knowledge of diuers wares in those countreyes.

Of the Kintal or hundred weight of Portingale, Spaine or France.

of the Kintal of Portingale.

Obserue besides these instructions following, to make diligent inquirie yourselfe, in all places where you trade, of euery of these pointes, for these notes may in some cōtries and through time be a litle altred and changed from the rules here set downe

NOTE that in Lisbon in Portingale, the kintall of pepper and of ginger (which they call the lesser kintal) is 112. pound. And their Roue or quarterne waight is 28. pound, and holdeth out with our English hundred of 112. pound, and sometimes two or thred [sic] pound more.

The kintal of most sorts of all other spices, as cloues, maces, nutmegs, Sinamōd, &c. cōtaineth 128. pound, and is called the great Kintal and the Roue containeth 32. pound, and doeth hold out about 15. or 16. pound more then our English hundred.

of the Kintal of Spaine

Note that in most parts of Spaine, their Kintal is, 100. li and con-

** Note that lead doth most comonly holde out after this rate of waight: but most sorts of other english wares, doe not so.*

taineth of our English waight but *102. li. So as our hundred waight is 10. in the 100. greater then theirs. Excepting the Kintal waight of Iron in Biskey, which is 150. pound, and doth make about 114. pound of our English waight.[40]

of the Kintal of France.

Note that in Rochel and Burdeaux, and so in most parts of France, the Kintal is 100. pound and holdeth out with our English hundred: sauing that through falshood of the wayers, it falleth lesse in one place then in another.

Of The Measvres Of cloth in Portingale, Spaine and Fraunce.

Portingale.

Note that the measure of cloth in Lisborne is the Couada: which conteineth about 3. quarters of our English yarde. But the measure of Linnen cloth, is chiefely bought and sold by the Vare: which is about an Ell lesse a naile of our English measure.[41]

Spaine.

Note that the measure of Spaine is called the Vare: which conteineth an English yard lesse a naile.

France.

Note that the measure of France, is the Aulne: which conteineth almost a naile longer than our English Ell.

Of the Measvres of Corne and Salt in Portingale, Spaine, and France

Portingale

** The Corn measure of Bristow is 8. gallonds Winchester.*

Note that the measure of corne in Lisborne is the Alquer: and 3. Alquers make about a Bushel of our Bristow measure, which is *8. gallonds Winchester: and 5. Alquers or neere thereabouts, maketh a Hanic of the measure of Spaine.

Spaine

Note that the measure of Spaine, is [the] Hannic,[42] which conteineth about a Bushell and a halfe of our measure of Bristow: so as 2. Hanicks make about 3. Bushels of ours.

France

Note that the measure of Rochel and Burdeaux is the Boiseau: which conteineth neere about 3. peckes of our Bristow measure.

Of the Measure of salt

Portingale

Item the measure of Salt of Portingale, is called the Muye: & 60. Alquers makes a Muye: [and] [43] 2. Muyes and 15. Alquers or thereabouts, makes a tonne of our water mesure of Bristow.

Spaine.

Item, the measure of Salt of Spain is called the Kayis, and 12. Hanicks goeth to a Kayis: And 2. Kayis and 3 Hanicks or thereabouts, makes a tun of our water measure of Bristow.

The water mesure of Salt of Bristow is 10. gallonds Winchester: & the tonne is 40. of those mesurs or bushels

France.

Item in Rochel in France, the measure of salt is the Boiseau: and 24. Boiseaus makes a Muy: and 28 Muyes maketh a hundred: & 2. Muyes makes about a tunne and 5. bushels of our Bristowe measure. The best measure of all is the Oldron measure, which is 36. Muyes to a hundred: and euery hundred maketh about 20. tunnes of our Bristow measure.

Of the Valve of Monies in Spaine, Portingale and France

Spaine

Note that the Ducket of Spain, hath 11. rials of plate: and eurie rial of plate hath 34. Meruedis: & euery Ducket 374. Meruedis. The Ducket * is 5. shillings sixpence of our English monie: the rial of

** Note that the Spanish ducket is so much in number; but more in value*

plate is sixpence, & the Meruede is lesse then our farthing. The halfe rial of plate is 17. Meruedis: and the quartel is 8. Meruedis and a halfe: and the single pistolet of gold is 11. Rials, 3. quartels being 400. Mereudis, which is 6. shillings lesse 3. halfepence of our English money.

Portingale

Note that the Ducket of Portingale is 10. Rials, and euerie Rial 40. Res: & euery Ducket 400. res. The Ducket is iust our English crowne: the Rial of plate is six pence: and the Res is about halfe a farthing. The Teston of Portingale is 2. Rials and a half, which is one shilling and three pence English: and the halfe Rial or Vinten is 20. Res, which is three pence English: and the Milres of gold is 1000. Res iust, which is two Duckets and halfe, and is twelue shillings six pence English.

France

Note that the French crowne of France called the Escu, is 3. Liuers: and euery Liuer 20. Sous: and euery Escu 60. Sous. The Escu is six shillings English mony: the Liuer is two shillings: and the Sous is almost one penny & farthing, for fiue Sous is sixpence English. The Sous also is deuided into Liardes and into Deniers: for there goeth to the Sous 6. Liards, & to the Liard 2. Deniers, and 12. Deniers to a Sous. The Flemish Crowne is 2. Sous lesse then is the French crowne. The Teston of France is 14. Sous and a halfe, which is one shilling fiue pence halfe penny: and some of the newer Testons are worth 15. Sous, which is one shilling and sixe pence English.

A BRIEFE INSTRVCTION FOR THE

Better Knowledge of certaine wares of Portingale, Spaine and France.

Pepper.

NOte that of pepper: the greatest and largest is best, & that which is cleanest without much dust. The which you shal trie the cleanenesse of it, by taking vp a handfull of it somewhat low in the bagge, for the dust will appeare on your fingers after letting downe the pepper. The russet coloured pepper is best, and that which is soūd: the which you may proue the soundnesse of it, by rubbing it hard betwixt your hands. If it be verie blacke of colour, and the dust of it moist, and sticking to your fingers, then hath it taken wet, and is not so good.

Cloues.

Note that of Cloues: the longest and smallest stems are best, and which are cleane without dust, & without much of the mother cloue & which are drie. The which you may proue the drinesse of them, by breaking the stems of some of them: that if they breake short and not bow, then is it a signe that they are good and drie. But if they be verie blacke, and will bend: then is it like they are moyst and wet.

Mases.

Note that of Maces: the greatest and largest are best, and which are of fayer and bright orenge colour, and [44] such as are cleanest and best without the nutmegs, and without the bright yellowe maces.

Sinamond

Note that of Sinamond, the largest and thinnest rinde is best, and those which are of fayer and bright orenge colour, and which are quickest and pleasantest on the tong. But the thicke rind & dusky colourd Sinamon is not so good.

Nutmegs.

Note that of Nutmegs, the largest and greatest are best, and which are of bright russet colour, and sound, waightie, and quicke on the tongue.

Ginger.

Note that of Ginger, the greatest and largest are best, and which are of yellow or faire russet colour, and sound, waightie, and hote on the tongue.

Suger.

Note that of Suger, the faire and white colour is best, and which is hard, and without brownnesse in the heart of the loafe: the which brownnesse of it is seene, by hauing the loafe broken in the midst, or otherwise if the whole head of the loafe round about be browne and darke coloured.

Calicowes

** Of Calicowes are diuers and sundry sortes: and therefore the knowledge of them al cannot be perfectly described*

Note that of Calicowes:* the whitest and cleanest without starch are best, and which are of fine thrid, close made, and that haue substance in feeling thē. But those which are much starched, of great thrid, and thine woven, are not so good.

Salt.

Note, that of Salt the brightest and whitest colour is best, & which is cleane without durte or strawes, and that which is old and not new salt. The which if it be new, it is perceaued by the moistnes of it, and by sticking of it to your fingers, after hard wringing of it in your hande.

Cochenele.

Note, that of Cochenele the largest & brightest gray or siluer colour is best, and that which doth cast the quickest & most orient red in the palme of your hand, after you haue rubbed and mingled it with a little spitle.

Oyles.

Note of Oyle, the sweetest, and clearest, yellowest, greenest, and without water or soot, is the best. But if it be darke coloured, very rank and with much soote, it is not good.

Sope.

Note that of Portingale Sope: the whitest, hardest, dryest, and swetest is best, and which hath most of the blew vains & the colour cleer & faire, & which (as I said) is hardest & driest. The which is somwhat perceaued, by the noise or ratling that it will make within the Searne when it is shaken. But if it be duskie coloured, of few blew vaines, soft, of greasie and rank sauour, moist, and clinging one to another, it is not so good.

Ode.[45]

Note that of Ode: the knowledge & goodnes thereof, is very hardly perceaued before it come to proofe of boiling, and men chuse it either by experience or good report of the Soyles where it groweth, or els of the fatnes of the ode. The which is somewhat perceaued the fatnes of it, by breaking a clot betwixt your fingers, wherin will apeere certaines vaines of thrids: the which vaines if they be many, and will spin long, it is a good signe: but if there be fewe or none, and do breake short, it is an euill sign. Also some vse triall of it, by rubbing it with a little spitle on a knife: the which if it doe cast a good quicke colour, & doth somewhat staine the knife: they say it is a good signe. &c.

Iron

Note that of Iron, the smallest and thinnest drawen, and which hath least crackes though most flawes, it is the best. And if in breaking a tong or barre, it do breake tough, & not short, it is good. But if it looke after a firy red colour, & hath many crackes, it is not good.

Traine.[46]

Note that of Traine: the clearest & swetest is best, and that which is without much soote or water. But if it be thicke and darke coloured and very ranke of fauour, it is not good.

Wines.

Of wines: it cannot be set downe by pen or words, the right knowledge of it, for it is perceiuable only by the taste and fauor. But the best sorts of wines generally are, when they doe tast pleasant and strong withall, and when they drinke cleane and quicke in the pallet of the mouth, and whē they are cleere & white hued if they be white Wines, or of faire orient red, if they be red wines. But if they drinke weake, rough, foule, flat, inclining to egernesse, or long: they are not good.

HERE FOLLOWETH

THE FORME OF A SPANISH AC-

compt, and howe to make a bill of la-
ding, a letter of remembrance, a bill of
exchange, a bill of debt, an acquittance
a letter of Atturney, an obligacion,
and a Policie for assu-
rance. &c.

Set this following as the superscription upon the Accompt.

THE ACCOMPT OF MY MASTER, ALDERMAN Aldworth marchant of the citie of Bristowe, giuen by me his seruant R.A. the sixteenth day of Ianuarie. 1589.

The 14. day of December 1589.

47

Broade clothes 10. *peeces and one fine Stammell: for the account of my Master Alderman Aldworth marchant of the cittie of Bristowe, marked vnder this marke in the margent, receiued out of the Gabriel in Lisbone: oweth these charges folowing.*	
For barkage, landing and other charges, which commeth to	*Nu.º* 1. *Res.*
4. *Rials* 5. *Res. Amount into Portingall Res.* o	ooo*M**ooo*V**165
For Marco custome[48] *at* 10. *Res the packe.* o	*V*.010
For measuring at 10. *Res the Cloth.* o	*V*.110
For wyndage at 20. *res the packe.* o	*V*.020
For brokerage[49] *at halfe per* 100. o	1.*V*.236
For aueredge[50] *at* 3 *Ri. the Cloth.* o	1.*V*.320
*For my *prouision*[51] *at* 2. *and a halfe per* 100.	6.*V*.180
The Neate hereof is 238.*V*.159 *Res: for which I will make you creditor in account currant. Fol.* 38 [*this edition, p.* 36].	ooo*M*.238.*V*.159
{ *Summe totall*	*Res* oo*M*.247.*V*.200

Note that this letter *M. standeth for Million, and this letter *V. standeth for thousand.

Obserue heere in the account of Sales: that you write first on the other side, what is due to your master and so shall you by sight of that, the better drawe out the Neate of the charges, and also of your customes, brokerage, and prouision.

Note that *prouision is not but in certaine degrees to be charged, nor Auerege.

The 14. day of December 1589.

Per contra: is due 247.*V*.200 *in the Sales of* 10 *fine brode clothes, and one Stammell, and a cotton wrapper: sold to Jaques Magomes Draper of Lisbone at* 53. *Duckets* 4. *Rials a cloth: & the Stammell at* 75. *duckets: and the cotton wrapper containing* 40. *couades, at* 2 *Rials* 10. *Res the couada, &c. amount*

{ *Summe totall*	*Res* 000*M*.247.*V*.200

The 18. day of December 1589.

Wax 14. *Kintals and* 9. *pound for the account of my master Alderman Aldworth: marked vnder this mark in the margent, and receiued out of the Gabriel in Lisbone: oweth these charges following.*

For barking, landing and other charges which cometh to 2. *Rials* 5. *Res. Amount into Portingall Res.* o.	*Res* ooo*M*.ooo*V*.085
For windage at 5, *Res the hogshed.* o.	*V*.040
For auerege at one Riall and a halfe per kintall	*V*.440
For brokerage at halfe per 100. o	*V*.662
For my prouision at 2. *and halfe per* 100. o	3*V*.312
*The *Neate heereof is* 127*V*.961 *Res: for which I will make creditor in account currant. Fol.* 38. o. [*this edition, p.* 36].	ooo*M*.127*V*.961
Summe totall	*Res* ooo*M*.132*V*.500[52]

*Summe all the charges in a wast paper, and then subtract it out of the totall in the other side: and the remainder thereof is the *Neate.

Note that the customes and dueties vpon wares in Portingall and Spaine, doth oftentimes change: therefore you must euerie voyage, make diligent inquirie of it, and so accordingly charge the account.

The 18. day of December 1589.

Per contra: is due 132.*V*.500. *Res in the Sales of* 14. *kintals and* 9. *pound of Wax, sold to Bernard Priget marchant of Lisbon at* 23. *Duckats* 5. *Rials the kintall. Amount.*

	Res
{ *Summe totall.*	000*M*.132.*V*.500[53]

The 28. day of December 1589

Lead 15. *Tunnes containing* 270. *peeces, for the account of my master Alderman Aldworth, marked vnder this marke in the margent, receiued out of the Ioseph in S. Lucar, oweth these charges following.*	
For barkage, landing, and other charges, which commeth to 2 *Duckats* 5. *Rials. Amount into Spanish Meruedis.* o	*Mer.* ooo*M*.ooo.*V*.918
For lodgeroom and waying it. Amount. o.	*V*.730
For windage at 17. *Mer. the Tunne.* o.	*V*.255
*For *custome at* 7. *and a halfe per* 100. o	16*V*.437
For brokerage at halfe per 100. o	1.*V*.096
For auerege at 3. *Rials per Tunne.* o	1.*V*.530
*For my *prouision at* 2. *and a halfe per* 100. o	5.*V*.484
The Neate here of is, 192.*V*.910 *Meruedis: for which I will make you creditor in Account currant. Folio.* 38 [*this edition, p.* 36].	ooo*M*.192.*V*.910
Summe totall.	ooo.*M*.219.*V*.360

The easiest rule to take out your custome or prouision vpon the 100. is onely to multiply your Totall by your number of 7. and a halfe,[54] or 2 & a halfe. And then for your halfe, take the halfe of your first summe and set it vnder your Multiplier, and so summe it vp altogither: and all sauing the 2. last figures, is your prouision or custome.

Example

219360
2½

438720
109680

5484|00

The 28. day of Ianuarie 1589 [55]

Per contra: is due 219.*V*.360. *Meruedis: in the sales of* 300. *Kintals and tenne poundes of lead: sold to Francisco Berea marchant of Siuill at* 21. *Rials,* 17, *Meruedis the Kintall*

{ *Summe totall*	*Mer* 000*M*.219.*V*.360

56

The 4. day of Ianuarie 1589.

Bayes 20. *peeces for the account of my master Alderman Aldworth, marked under this marke in the margent, receiued out of the Pleasure in S. Lucar: oweth charges following*

For barkage, landing, and other charges, which commeth to 4. *Rials. Amount into Spanish Meruedis.* o	*Nu.* 1. *Mer* 000*M*.000*V*.136
For lodge roome and carriage. o.	*V*.086
For custome at 7 *and a halfe per* 100. o	7*V*.346
For windage at 17. *Mer. the Packe.* o	*V*.017
For Auerege at 1. *Rial and a halfe the peece.* o.	1.*V*.020
For brokerage at halfe per 100. o	*V*.489
For my prouision at 2. *and halfe per* 100. o	2*V*.548
The Neate hereof is, 86.*V*.318 *Meruedis: for which I will make you creditor in Account currant. Folio* 46 [*this edition, p.* 44].	000*M*.086.*V*.318
Summe totall	*Mer.* 000*M*.097.*V*.960

The 4. day of Ianuarie 1589.[57]

Per contra: is due 97.*V*.960 *Meruedis: in the sales of* 20 *peeces of Bayes, solde to Pedro Meris Draper of S. Lucar at* 13 *Dukats* 4. *Rials a peece. Amount.*

{ *Summe totall.*	000*M*.097.*V*.960 *Mer.*

The 15. day of December 1589 [58]

Pepper for the account of my master Alderman Aldworth, marchant of the citie of Bristowe, oweth 124.*V*.800.*Res for* 6 *kintals laden in the Gabriel of Bristow, which cost the first penny* 52. *Dukats the kintall. Amount.* o.	*Res* 000*M*.124.*V*.800
(*More oweth these charges following.*)	
For 16. *Vares of Canuas to double bagge the pepper, at* 65. *Res the vare.* o.	1.*V*.040
For carriage and barkage. o.	*V*.090
For custome at the portage at 9. *Res per kintall.*	*V*.054
For custome at the India house at one per 100.	1.*V*.248
For windage. Amount. o.	*V*.017
For brokerage at halfe per 100. o.	*V*.624
For auerege at 80. *Res the bagge.* o.	*V*.240
For Dispacho in the portage cost 10. *Res.* o.	**V*.010
For my prouision at* 2. *and a halfe per* 100. o	3.*V*.203
{ *Summe totall.*	*Res* 000*M*.131.*V*.326

Heere nowe in the impliments obserue to write downe first your master dettor, for the charges of those wares which you lade him.

* Note here that in taking your * prouision: you must summe all the Items before, and so of the totall take it out.

Marchants Aviso | *Impliments*

The 15. day of December. 1589 [59]

Per contra: is due 131.*V*.326. *Res, in the whole charges of* 6. *Kintals of pepper marked vnder this marke in the margent: and bought of Michaell Sebra marchant of Lisbon, at* 52. *Duckats* (*sic*) *per Kintall.*[60] *Amount.*

{ *Summe totall.* 000*M*.131.*V*.326

The 16. day of December. 1589 [61]

**Cloues 2 kintals, and *Mases 3 Roues: and *Sinamon one kintall 2. Roues: for the account of my master Alderman Aldworth, oweth* 103.*V*.220 *Res, which cost the first pennie* 75. *Duckats* 4. *Rials the kintall of Cloues: and* 83 *Duckats the kintall of Mases, &* 68 *Duckats the kintall of Synamon. Amount.* 0.	*Res* 000*M*.103.*V*.220
(*More oweth these charges following.*)	
For 10. *Vares of Canuas to double bagge the spices at* 65. *Res the vare.* 0.	*V*.650
For carriage and barkage. 0.	*V*.120
For custome at the portage at 20. *Res per kintall*	*V*.080
For custome at the India house at one per 100. 0.	1.*V*.032
For windage at 5. *Res the bagge.* 0.	*V*.010
For auerege at 80. *Res the bagge.* 0.	*V*.240
For brokerage at halfe per 100. 0.	*V*.516
For prouision at 2. *and a halfe per* 100. 0.	2.*V*.646
{ *Summe totall.*	*Res* 000*M*.108.*V*.514

*Note that if you lade any great quantitie of diuers sorts of spices: then is it conuenient that you charge and make an account of euery one seuerally by itself. But if you buy but a small quantitie of ech sort: then for breuitie & ease of trouble, you may obserue that forme aboue prescribed, for the charge thereof will not be great, and euerie Marchant can quicklie guesse the seuerall charge.

The 16. day of December. 1589

Per contra: is due 108.*V*.514. *Res in the whole charges of* 2. *kintals of Cloues*: 3 *Roues of Mases*: *& one kintall* 2. *Roues of Synamon: laden in the Gabriel vnder this marke in the margent: and bought of Lewis Betron and Martin Ferbuc marchants of Lisborne*

{	*Summe totall.*	*Res* 000*M*.108.*V*.514

The 3. Day of Ianuarie 1589

Oyles 10. *pipes for the account of my master Alderman Aldworth, oweth* 115.*V*.600 *Meruedis for* 400. *Roues of Oyle, which cost the first penny* 8. *Rials and a halfe the Roue. Amount.* o	*Mer* 000*M*.115.*V*.600
(*More oweth these charges following*)	
For 10. *leare pipes*[62] *for the Oyles, which cost* 24. *Rio. and a halfe the Pipe. Amount into Spanish Meruedis.* o.	8.*V*.330
For watring the Pipes, and carriage of them at 15. *Mer. the Pipe.* o.	*V*.150
For Marco almeran: and bota fuera,[63] *at* 25. *Mer. the pipe.*	*V*.250
For S. Georges custome at one Riall per Tunne. o	*V*.170
For yeffo [*sic*] *for the Pipes at* 10. *Mer. the Pipe.* o	*V*.100
For carriage of them to the Shrof. [*sic*] *at* 21. *Mer. the Pipe.*	*V*.210
For filling, rowling and hooping of them, at 45. *Mer. the Pipe.* o.	*V*.450
For the Coopers wages at 3. *Rials the day, being* 5 *dayes.*	*V*.510
For Nailes, Corke, Canuas, and Leather.	*V*.170
For Incomiendo[64] *at one per* 100. o	1.*V*.156
For brokerage at halfe per 100. o	*V*.578
For cartage at 5. *Rials the Tunne.*	*V*.850
For barkage at 7. *Rials* 12. *Mer. the Tunne.*	1.*V*.250
For hooping againe aboorde the shippe at 17 *Mer. the Pipe*	*V*.170
For hundage at one Riall per Tunne	*V*.170
For windage at 17. *Mer. the Tunne*	*V*.085
For auerege at 3. *Rials per Tunne*	*V*.510
For my prouision at 2. *and halfe per* 100. o	3.*V*.267
Summe Totall	*Mer* 000*M*.133.*V*.976

Note that the customes and dueties vpon wares in Spaine and Portingale doe oftentimes change: therefore you must euery voyage, make diligent inquirie of it, and so accordingly charge the account.

The 3. day of Ianuarie 1589.

Per contra: is due 133.*V*.976. *Meruedis: in the whole charges of* 5. *Tunnes of Oyles containing* 400. *Roues: laden aboord the Gabriel in S. Lucar in Andolosia under this marke in the margent: and bought of Sebastian de Lega, Gentleman of Cyuell. Amount.*

{ *Summe totall.*	*Mer* 000*M*.133.*V*.976

The 5. day of Ianuarie 1589.

Secks for the account of my master Alderman Aldworth, oweth 89.*V*.760 *Meruedis, for* 20. *Buttes, which cost the first pennie* 12. *Duckats the Butt.*	*Mer* 000*M*.089.*V*.760
(*More oweth these charges following*)	
For custome in Sheeres at 7. *and a halfe per* 100	6.*V*.630
For imposition at 15. *Mer. the Butt.* o.	*V*.300
For Cartage to Portall at 4. *Ri. the Butt.* o	2.*V*.720
For hooping, barring, and other charges, at 25. *Mer. the Butt.* o.	*V*.500
For nayles, corke, and canuas, at 8. *Meruedis the Tunne.*	*V*.080
For Almerant at 14. *Mer. the Butt.* o.	*V*.280
For brokerage at one Riall the Butt. o.	*V*.680
For hundage at one Rial the Tunne. o.	*V*.340
For barkehyre at 7. *Rials the Tunne* o.	2.*V*.380
For custome to S. Georges chappell at 6. *Mer. the Butt.* o.	*V*.120
For Auerage at 3. *Rials the Tunne.* o.	1.*V*.020
For vllaging aborde the shippe,[65] *which came to* 187. *Mer. the Butt.* o.	3.*V*.740
For windage at 17. *Mer. the Tunne.*	*V*.170
For my prouision at 2. *and a halfe per* 100. o	2.*V*.788
Summe totall.	*Mer* 000*M*.111.*V*.508

The 5. day of Ianuarie 1589.

Per contra: is due 111.*V*.508 *Meruedis: in the whole charges of* 20 *Buttes of Secke, laden aboorde the Mynnion in S. Lucar in Andolozia, vnder this marke in the margent: and bought of Martin de Leso citizen of Sheres.*

{ *Summe totall.*	*Mer* 000*M*.111*V*.508

The 10. day of Ianuarie. 1589

My master Alderman Aldwoorth, merchant of the cittie of Bristow, oweth 131.V.326 Res of Portugal monies, which being reduced into Spannish Meruedis make 123.V.118. Mer. for so much cost with all charges of 6 kintals of Pepper as appeareth more at large, Folio 34 [this edition, p. 32].	Mer 000M.123.V.118
More oweth 108.V.514 Res, which in Spanish Meruedis is 101.V.731 Mer. for so much cost with all charges 2 Kintals of Cloues: 3. Roues of Mases, & one kintall 2. Roues of Synamon, as appeareth more at large Fol. 35 [this edition, p. 33].	000.M.101.V.731
More, oweth 133 V. 976 Mer. for so much cost with all charges 10. pipes of Oyle: as appeareth more at large: Fol. 36 [this edition, p. 34].	000.M.133.V.976
More oweth 111.V.508 Meruedis, for so much cost with all charges 20 Buttes of Sacke, as appeareth more at large. Fol. 37 [this edition, p. 35].	000.M.111.V.508
More oweth 914. Meruedis for registring the billes of exchange in Cyuill, and recouering the monies which is one Meruedi upon the Ducket. 0.	000.M.000V.914
More oweth 10 V.608. Mer. which is 28 Ds. 4. Res, for so much cost all my charges and expences of the voyage, as appeareth by the particular account thereof, which I will deliuer you. 0	000.M.010.V.608
Item 140. V.610. Mer. (which is 376. Duckets lesse 14. Meru) resteth to ballance this account: for the which I will be countable vnto you at the sight hereof.	000.M.140V.160
Summe total	000M.622V.465

Note heerein the account currant: that you must bring all your portingall (Res) into Spanish (Meruedis) which is onely to multiplie your some of Res, by the number of
Mul. 15 15. and so to diuide the multiplier of that, by the number of
Deu. 16 16 and that maketh it into Meruedis. This is a principall rule, & it were too long to yeeld the plaine reason of it. But note withall, that you must account after 375. Mer. to the spanish Ducket: which one Meruede is commonly allowed to the Factor of the recouer of the monies.

Marchants Aviso	*Account Currant*
The 10. day of Ianuarie 1589.	
My master Alderman Aldworth marchant of the cittie of Bristowe, is due 238 *V.* 159 *Res of Portingall monies: which being reduced into Spanish Meruedis, maketh* 223 *V*.274 *Meruedis, and is the Neate of* 10. *fine brode clothes, one Stammell and a wrapper: as appeareth more at large, Fol.* 30 [*this edition, p.* 28].	*Mer* 000.*M*.223.*V*.274
More is due 127.*V*.961. *Res. which in Spanish Meruedis is* 119.*V*.963 *Mer. and is the Neate of* 14. *kintals and* 9. *li of Waxe: as appeareth more at large. Folio.* 31.0 [*this edition, p.* 29].	000.*M*.119.*V*.963
More is due 192.*V*.910. *Meruedis, and is the neate of* 300 *Kintals and* 10. *pound of Lead, as appeereth, Folio.* 32 [*this edition, p.* 30].	000.*M*.192.*V*.910
More is due 86.*V*.318 *Meruedis: and is the neate of* 20 *peeces of Bayes, as appeareth, Fol.* 33 [*this edition, p.* 31].	000.*M*.086*V*.318
{ *Summe totall.*	*Mer* 000.*M*.622.*V*.465

Note that you still obserue, to keepe a copie of euerie marchants account that you deale for: for so will it be auailable for you, if you should be called in question againe, about your account.

{ Thus endeth the Account }

CONSTANTINI CRVX.

Here followe certaine points necessarie for young beginners.

A briefe order for making of a bill of lading, the which may serue for diverse mens goods, and may be sent to one Marchant alone, and request him to giue aduertisement of it to the others

HAth* laden by the grace of God in good safetie in Lisbon in Portingale, and in S. Lucar in the prouince of Andalouzia in Spaine: by R.A. marchant of the citie of Bristow, abord the ship called the *Pleasure*, wherof is maister for the present voyage W.M.[66] and bound for the Port of Bristowe in England, these goods & marchandise following Namely, 5. bags of pepper containing 12. Kintals and 2 Roues: for the accompt of my master T.R.[68] marchant of the citie of Bristowe, and marked vnder this marke in the margent. More 10. pipes of oile for his accompt, marked also with the former marke. More 20. buts of Secke for his accompt, marked also with the former marks.

**Note here that you obserue to make still a seuerall bill of lading for your masters goods: and not to vse this forme and order, but when your hast of busines is great, or when you lade but some small cabo[67] for a Marchant*

More also 3. Roues of Cochenele for the accompt of master I.B.[69] marchant of Bristowe, and marked as in the margent. More 5 buts of seck for his accompt, marked with the former marke.

More 8 buts of Secke for the accompt of maister T.I.[70] marchant of Bristow, and marked as in the margent.[71] All which goods and marchandises, I R.A. purser of the said ship do acknowledge to haue receaued aborde, well and sufficiently condicioned. And by these presents I do bind my selfe with the ship, her apparell and freight, to deliuer the said goods in iust order and condition againe vnto the marchants and owners aforsaid, God sending the ship and goods to her Port in safetie.[72] In witnesse of truth I R.A. Purser haue vnto* two of these billes of lading set my hand, giuen the 20. day Ianuarie 1589.

**Note that [you] are to make either 2. or 3 of these billes[73]*

By me R.A.

A briefe order for making a marchants particular remembrance

**These words have relation to the Generall remembrance spoken of in the beginning.*

A Remembrance for you my seruant R.A. that principally you do with diligēce *read & regard the counsel of that litle booke which I now geue you. And now (God willing) at your coming to Lisbon, you shal receaue out of the Ioseph wherin you go, one pack of 10. fine brode Clothes, and 1. fine stamell cloth, with a gray cotten wraper, the which are marked as in the margent.[74] The brode clothes stand me with all charges twelue pounds a cloth, and I hope they will yeld you in Lisbon about 52. duckets. The Stāmel standeth me in 17. pound, and I hope will yeeld you 75. Duckets: & the wrapper cost 30. shillings. All which doe you your best indeuoure, to sell as the time serueth. More (God willing) you shall receiue 3. Hogshead of waxe, marked also with the former marke, wherein is 14. hundred and 13. pound. It doth stand me all charges about 5. pound 12. shillings the hundreth: the which you may sell for 25. Duckets a Kintal, if the time so offereth. More also you shall receaue for my acompt 20 tunnes of lead, conteining 345. peeces marked as in the top of the former page:[75] the which if you cannot sel to some reckning in Lisbon, do you let it goe along in the Ship to S. Lucar, and there to sell it as well as you may: I hope it will be worth 22. Rials the Kintall.

And now for my impliments, do you lade me in the Ioseph 8. Kintals of good and large pepper, and se that it be well made vp in good bagges, & giue charge it may be stowed in the driest part of the ship. More at your coming to S. Lucar, do you lade me in the Gabriel 5. tuns of good oyles: and do you see well both to the watring and hooping of your caske, and to the cleannes of the Oyle that it be without soote. More do you also lade in the Vnicorne 12. pipes of Oyle, and haue care vnto it as before I haue said. More lade me in the same ship the Vnicorne 16. Buts of very good Secke and do you giue a Ducket or two the more in a But, to haue them principall good. And if after you haue bought al these wares, there be any surplus money remaining: do you bestow it in good Cochenele, so farr as it will rise, and marke all these goods with my marke as is before in the margent. But if it fall out that you shall want any monies to furnish the lading of 15. tunnes in the Vnicorne, which I am bounde vnto: thē request so much friēdship of T.M. to furnish that which you want, in monyes by exchang: and agree with him for the exchange so good cheape as you can, as about 6. shillings and 4. pens or 6. shillings and 8. pens the Ducket, and this my letter shall be your warrant. Make master W.O. in Lisbon, and master I.T. in S. Lucar, your friends to ayd and instruct you, in the buying and selling of all your wares: and giue thē that thing, which I deliuered you, for a token of goodwill from me. Inquire secretly what wares are in good request & best vendible: and send me speedy and secret intelligence of it. See that the Purser of the Vnicorne firme your billes of lading. Thus exhorting you to remember your duety towardes God: whom I beseech to protect you euermore by his holy Spirit, and prosper you in all your affaires. Bristow this 17. of December. An. 1589.

Your Master to doo you any good that you shall deserue.

T.A.

The forme of a bill of exchange for the countrey of Spaine.

WOrshipfull: may it please you to pay vpon this my first bill vnto R.N. or the bearer hereof, within 15. dayes after the safe arriual of the Gabriell of Bristow to her Port of discharge: *thirtie and three pounds, sixe shillings and eight pence. Which is for 100. Duckets that I haue vp by exchange for your vse of T.M. a marchant of London at six shillings and eight pence the Ducket. From S. Lucar the 16. day of December, 1589

**Note that you must make 3. of these billes.*

**Thirty and thre pound six shillings and eight pence*

By me R.A.

Say as foloweth in your second bil of exchange, and so accordingly in the third.

WOrshipful: may it please you to pay vpon this my second bill (my first not being payed) vnto R.N. or the bearer hereof: and so foorth as in the other

A bill of Exchange to be made in England.[76]

WItnesseth this present bill of exchange: that I R.A. marchant of the citie of Bristowe, do owe vnto T.M. marchant of the sayd citie, the summe of 100. Duckets: I say an hundred Duckets of currant monie of Spaine, accompting after 11. rials of plate to the Ducket. To be payd vnto the said T.M. or his assignes, within 10. dayes next and immediately after the safe arriuall of the good ship called the Gabriel of Bristowe, to the port of S. Lucar in Andalouzia in Spaine, or any other porte of hir discharge. And for the true payment thereof, I the abouenamed RA. do binde me, my goods my heirs executors, & assignes, firmly to these presents. In witnesse of the truth, I haue caused two of these billes to be made (the which the one being payed, the other to be voide): and haue put my firme and seale vnto them, & deliuered them as my deed, in Bristow the 15. day of September 1589. and in the 31. yeare of our Soueraigne, Queene Elizabeth her maiesties raigne, &c.

An aquittance

WItnesseth these presents: that I R.A. marchant of the city of Bristow, haue receaued of T.M. marchant of the said city, the summe of a 100. Duckets currant monies of Spaine, due vnto my master T.A. as apeared by a bill of exchange. Wherefore to testify that I am truely satisfied & payd of the aforsaid summe: I haue vnto this aquittance set my firme, and deliuered it as my deed the 18. day of Nouember. 1589.

By me R.A.

A bill of Atturney

WItnesseth these presents that I R.A. marchant of the City of Bristow, do substitute and appoint my true & lawful atturney T.M. marchant of Bridgwater: to recouer & receaue of G.H. marchāt of the aforesaid City of Bristow the summe of 25. pound, due vnto me as appeareth by his bil. Wherfore I giue also to the said T.M, all my owne full power and authority, to deale and to do as in steed of my self. In witnesse of the truth, I haue vnto this present bill of Atturney, put my firme and seale, & deliuered it as my deed, in Bristow the 17. day of Nouember 1589, and in the 32. yeare of our Soueraigne, Queene Elizabeth her Maiesties Raigne. &c.

A bill of debt

BE it known vnto all mē by these presents: that I R.A. marchant of the Citie of Bristowe owe vnto T.M. marchant of the said City: the summe of 25. pounds 8. shillings, of good & currant moneys of England, to be payd vnto the said T.M. or his assignes, at or vpon the 25. day of July next ensuing the date hereof. And for the true payment thereof: I the aboue named R.A. do binde me, my goods, heirs, executors, administrators, and assignes, firmely by these presents. In witnesse of truth I haue caused this bill of debt to be made, and haue hereunto put my firme and seale, and deliuered it as my deede, in Bristow the 4. day of May 1589. and in the 31. yeare of our Soueraigne, Queene Elizabeth her Maiesties Reigne, &c.

A Bond or Obligacion

Nouerint universi per praesentes me R.A. de ciuitate Bristoliae mercatorē, teneri & firmiter obligari T.M. de eadem ciuitate Mercatori: in viginti libris bonae & legalis monetae Angliae. Soluendis eidem T.M. aut suo certo Atturnato executoribus, siue administratoribus suis. Ad quam quidem solutionem bene & fideliter faciendam, obligo me, heredes, executores & administratores meos, firmiter per praesentes. Sigillo meo sigillatum, datum septimo die Nouembris, anno regni Dominae nostrae Elizabethae, Dei gratia Angliae, Franciae, & Hyberniae Reginae, fidei defens. &c. tricesimo primo.

THe condition of this Obligacion is such, that if the aboue bounden R.A. his heires, executors or assignes, doe well and truly content and pay, or cause to be contented and payd, vnto the aboue named T.M. his executors, administrators or assignes, the summe of tenne pounds of good and currant money of England, on the sixteenth day of May next insuing the date aboue written, without couen or fraude: That then this obligacion to be void, or else to stand in full force and vertue.

A Policie or writing of assurance

IN the name of God Amen. Be it known vnto all men by these presents: that Thomas Aldsworth marchant of the citie of Bristowe doth make assurance and causeth himselfe to be assured from the Port of the sayd citie of Bristow called Hungrode [77] vnto the port of Lisbon in the kingdome of Portingale, and therehence directly backe againe to the aforesayd Port of Bristow: vpon the bodie, tackle, apparell, ordinance, munition, artillerie, boate, and other furniture, of the good ship called the Gabriell of Bristow, of the burthen of 60. tunnes, or thereabouts. And also vpon all goods, wares, and marchandises laden or to be laden in the aforesayd ship the Gabriel, whereof is maister vnder God for this present voyage R.M. or by what other name the maister of the ship may or shal be called. Beginning the aduenture from the day and houre of the lading of the anker, spreading the sayle, and departure of the sayde ship from Hungrode aforesaid. And so shall continue and endure vntill such time as the said ship with all her sayd furniture, & all the goods and marchandises laden in her, shall returne and safely arriue back againe from Lisbon vnto the Port of Hungrode aforesayd, & there hath surged and mored [78] at an anker by the space of 24. houres in good safetie. Touching the aduentures and perils which we the assurers hereafter named are contented to beare and take vpon vs this present voyage, are of the seas, men of warre, fire, enemies, pirats, rouers, theeuves, Iettesons, letters of marke and countermarke, arrests, restraints, and detainments of Kings and Princes & of all other persons, barratry of the Master and mariners, and of all other perils, losses, & misfortunes whatsoeuer they be, or howsoeuer to the damage or hurt of the sayd Ship and goods or any part or parcell thereof. And that in case of any misfortunes: it shall then be lawfull to the assured his factor, seruant, or assigne, to sue labour, & trauail, for in and about, the defence, safgard and recouerie of the said Ship & goods, and all other the premisses, without any preiudice to this assurance. To the charges whereof, we th'assurers shal contribute eche one according to the rate and quantity of his summe herein assured. It is to be vnderstood that this present writing and assurance shallbe of as much force, strength &

effect, as the best and most surest policie or writing of assurance which hath bene euer heretofore vsed to be made in Lumbard streete, or now within the Roial exchange in London. And so we the assurers are contented, and doe promise and bind our selues and euerie of vs, our heirs, executors and assignes [79] for the true performance of the premises, according to the vse and custome of the said streete, or Royall exchange. Confessing our selues to be fully satisfied and paied of and for the considerations due vs after the rate of 7. upon the 100. And in testimony of the truth, we the assurers haue hereunto seuerally subscribed our names and summes of money assured, giuen in London the 19. day of September. 1589.

I W.N. marchant of London am content with this assurance (which God preserue) for 25. pounds this 19. day of September. 1589. 25.*li*

I R.T. marchant of London am content with this assurance (which God preserue) for 25. pounds this 20. day of September. 1589. 25.*li*

I M.R. marchant of Bristow am content with this assurance (which God) preserve for 15. pounds [80] this 21. day of September 1589. 25.*li*

CONSTANTINI CRVX.

HERE FOLLOWE CERTAINE GODLY SENTENCES

necessarie for a youth to meditate vpon.[81]

FIrst seeke the kingdome of God and the righteousness thereof: and then all things shall be giuen thee that thou hast neede of.

Apply thy selfe vnto labour while thou art young, lest in thine old age thy body become full of diseases, and they ende be in reproch and pouertie.

The godly and diligent man shall haue prosperitie in all his wayes; but he that followeth pleasure and voluptuousnesse, shall haue much sorrow before he die.

Take heed of vsing a false ballance or measure, for it is an abhomination before God: and a swearing and lying tongue, maketh hote the curse of God vpon his house.

Couet not ouermuch familiaritie amongst men: for it maketh thee spend much losse of time.

Let not thy expences be equall with thy gaynes: for either sicknes, naughtie dettors, let of trade, and misfortune by the sea or land, may soone ouerthrow thee.

Linke not in amity with too many mē that are aboue thy calling: for it will much increase thy trouble and charge.

Beware in any case of suertiship: for it maketh thy friend thine enemy; it indangereth thy estate; and impaireth thy owne credit.

Be not hasty in giuing credit to euery man; but take heed to a man that is ful of words, that hath red eyes, that goeth much to law, and that is suspected to liue vnchaste.

When thou promisest any thing: be not slacke to performe it, for he that giueth quickly, giueth double.

If either of good will or necessity thou must doe a thing, see thou do it gladly & cheerfully: for so shall thy gift be well accepted, & thy labour and cost neuer a whit the more.

Remember often thy Creator, and how he hath made the whol compasse of the day and night to serue thee, but thee to serue only him. Wherefore it thou requite not thy maker, to serue him one houre or little momēt of the day, for foure and twenty houres which he serueth thee: for thy beastly vnthankfulnes thou hast lost both thy light in this world, and shalt find darknes in the world to come.

If thou wilt prosper pray: if thou wil haue blessinges, restore what thou hast euill gotten: if thou wilt haue ioye of thy labours, be single in thy tongue and eye, vse no lying nor deceit.

Thinke it not inough to refraine thee from doing euill: but know that it is also thy dutie to do that which is good. Therefore be feruēt for the praise of thy Creator: geue good example: put forwards thy Children & seruants in the seruice of God: help the widow, the fatherlesse, the stranger, the poore, and the oppressed.

Do vnto another as thou wouldest be done to thy selfe: and offer not that vnto another, which thy self wouldest take in offence.

Be not greedy nor in lust after that, which is both displeasant vnto God; hurtfull to thy body; an enemy to thy soule; and a shortner of thy life: which is, Wine, Wealth and Women.

What winneth a man by whordome? euen but a momentany pleasure; a present sorrow to his minde; a perpetuall sicknes to his bodie, and eternall damnation (without hartie repentance and amendment) to his soul.

What profiteth a man by deceit, forswearing, and dissimulation? he heapeth to himselfe the horrible vengeance of God? [!] and seruantes who shall serue him the like; and offereth his soule as a pray vnto Sathan.

What auayleth it a man to fare delicately & to drink much of pleasant & strong drinks? His mouth receaueth twise so much bitternesse as it had before delight; he shall become corrupt as the Tode, and shall returne to vomite with the dogge.

What getteth a man by lying? Not to be beleeued when he speaketh trueth.

Feare God: for he can destroy both thy bodie and soule.

Honor thy Prince: for she hath power ouer life and death.

Loue thy parents: for they are the best friēds thou shalt euer haue.

Giue reuerence to thy betters: for therein thou shalt haue honor to thyselfe.

Be curteous and lowly to all men: for thereby thine enemies report shal be doubted of.

Be not wise in thine owne conceipt: for thou canst not know all thine owne imperfections.

Be not carefull to please thine eye: for it is the deceiptfullest enemie thou hast.

Remember who made thee: it was God. Remember of what thou wast made: euen of earth and clay. Remember wherfore thou wast made: to honor and glorifie God. Remember to what thou shalt be made: euen to dust and ashes. Remember to what thou mayst be made againe: euen a glorious and immortall bodie.

Whoso taketh vpon him the degree of a seruant, let these three things bee his chiefest thought and meditation. The first, that euerie morning and euening, he performe his dutifull obedience and thankesgiuing, by his prayers vnto God. The Second, that he always carie in mind, what carefulnesse, truth, and diligence, is required in his seruice towards his maister. The third, how hee himselfe may liue with honestie and credit in time to come.

THE CONCLVSION, WHICH IS *an historie very profitable and delightful for a youth to reade and meditate.*

THere was a certaine Philosopher, who lying on his death bed, called his sonne, & sayd these wordes vnto him. My sonne when I thy father am dead, remember me by recompting often vnto thyselfe this counsell which now I giue vnto thee. First learne of the little singing birds, who neuer misse in the morning and at euening, but in their kinde, they yeeld foorth their voices in praise and reioycing of their Creator and maker: and so see that thou also doo neuer forget & neglect the same.

Learn of the litle emet that prouideth in the sommer her foode for the winter: and so see that thou also in thy youth, labor for thy maintenance against thine age. Learne of the cocke, that often watcheth and croweth in the night, both to preserue himself and his fellowes from the wesell: and see that thou often watch, and stretch forth thy voice in prayer by night vnto God, and in that quiet time, studie to preuēt thy dangers. Learne of the litle dog, who because he is the humblest creature of all vnto man, is therfore most loued and esteemed: & so see that thou euermore shew thyselfe humble & lowly vnto euery man. Learne of the silk worm, who as soone as she gathereth strength to yeeld anie vertue frō her, neuer ceasseth nor waxeth wearie vntil she die: and so see that thou also contēt not thyself, to do thy duty to God and man for a time, (as most men do) but still continue in vertue till thy verie liues end.

Thus my son (quoth he) if thou wilt obey this my counsell, it shall alwayes goe well with thee: but contrariwise if thou forsake it, & follow thine owne imaginations, it will happen vnto thee according to this example. There dwelt by a forest side a shepheard, who to preserue his sheep from a lion, which oftentimes had caried them away for a pray to his whelp, prepared many snares and engines to destroy this lion: but the old liō perceauing these traps to be layd for him, departed with his yong one to another forrest. But when the whelp grewe to be as big a lion as his father, he thus saith vnto him: Father, methinks I can remember that this place is not the cuntrey where I was born, what then was the cause that made thee to depart therehence? Saith the old lion, my sonne it is not indeed our natiue cuntrey: but there is a little dwarf a man dwelling in that place, whō for his subtle traps that he laid to take from me my life, I feared, and so fled therehence. Saith the young lion: and I sweare by my beard that I will be reuenged of him, and will go now and teare him in peeces with my teeth. Nay (sayth the old lion) do not so, for if I myselfe could not possibly get reuēge against him, thou canst not in any sort do it. But the yong lion would not be ruled by his father, but goeth vnto this forest where the shepheard dwelt: who finding him within his house & the dores shut, called vnto him and sayd: O thou naughtie & vile wretch, why has thou so abused my father, as to driue him from his natiue countrey, ouer which & all the beasts thereof, he raigned as king: I tell thee that I his sonne wilbe reuenged of thee for making him so to lose his right. The man being within his house stoutly answered: I regard not a rush either thee or thy father, but if thou once offer to enter my doores, I haue here both my staff and my axe to beate & to cut thee in peeces. The yong lion was straightwayes amazed at his stout wordes, and sayde: then come thou forth, and go with me to yonder moyle, and let him be iudge betwixt thee & me, whether thou hast done my father wrōg or not. Saith the shepheard: if thou wilt adiure and sweare to de me no harme, I will go with thee. So the yong lion sware vnto him to doe him no harme. The man then leadeth the way vnto the lion, by those engins that he had prepared long before: and anon the yong lion fell into one of his pits, and was entangled by his 2 forefeet. O (saith the Lion) helpe me, for I know not what is this that hath bound my feet uerie fast together. Saith the shepheard, I am not able to helpe thee, but tary thou here, and I will go and cal hether the moile. But the lion as well as he could, did yet get forth of the pit, & went iumping and leaping to follow after the man. By and by againe he fel into another pit, wherby his two hinder leggs were also caught fast. The shepheard now seeing him well tyed and bound: he then cutteth with his knife a good greene staffe, & beginneth to lay blows strōgly vpon the lion.

The lion then remembred his father, and said to the man: O beat me not on my back nor my belly, but rather beate me on mine eares & on my heart: because with mine eares I would not heare the counsel of my father, nor with my heart would not beleeue it, when he said thou hadst more subtlety to preuaile, then I had strength. So the man beat him so long, both on the eares & the heart, that in the end he killed him. Euen so (saith the Philosopher to his sonne) will destructiō come vpon those which shall not accept & obey the good counsell & instructions of their aged fathers.[82]

FINIS

NOTES TO THE TEXT

1. Thomas Aldworth was one of the most distinguished Bristol merchants in the second half of the 16th century. He was a member of the Common Council from 1566 to 1594, and alderman from 1591 to 1599. He was sheriff in 1566–67, and Mayor of Bristol 1582–83, 1589, and 1592–93. He died on 25 February 1599 (A. B. Beaven, *Bristol Lists*, Bristol, 1899). For his interest in exploration and his correspondence with Sir Francis Walsingham, see Richard Hakluyt, *The Principal Navigations*, etc., Glasgow, 1905, VIII, 132–34. He was concerned in privateering and owned the *Gabriel*, 80 tons, in 1593, together with Robert Aldworth and Edmund Browne (J. W. Damer Powell, *Bristol Privateers and Ships of War*, Bristol, 1930, pp. 48, 343). He was one of the three Bristol Assistants of the Spanish Company in its charter of 1577 (V. M. Shillington and H. B. Wallis Chapman, *The Commercial Relations of England and Portugal*, London, n.d., p. 317). Thomas Aldworth was associated with John Browne in 1576 when the *Peter* of Bristol was shipwrecked and its rich cargo fell into the hands of some of the inhabitants of Somerset, Cornwall, and South Wales (*Acts of the Privy Council*, 1575–77, p. 113). In 1593 when Aldworth was Mayor of Bristol he, together with John Browne and Robert Kitchen, wrote to Burleigh recommending John Dowle for a customer's place at Bristol (*Cal. S.P. Domestic* 1591–94, p. 347). There is a copy of his will in the Bristol Record Office (*Great Orphan Books* III. 64 (v) ff). For his monumental tablet in St. Mark's Chapel, Bristol, see William Barrett, *The History and Antiquities of the City of Bristol*, Bristol, 1789, pp. 350–51.

2. It is not clear whether this refers to the merchants in general or to a particular company of merchants. For a discussion of merchant organizations in Bristol in the later 16th century, see Patrick McGrath, *Records relating to the Society of Merchant Venturers of the City of Bristol in the Seventeenth Century*, Bristol Record Society, vol. XVII, 1952, pp. XII–XVI.

3. Abbreviation signs were often used in this 1589 edition, and are reproduced in this present reprinting.

4. Possibly the author feared that the importation of printed works into Spain from an heretical country might be prohibited.

5. Printed as "J.B." in the edition of 1591.

6. In the editions after 1591, the date "1587" was added at the end of this note. Presumably this was not necessary in the early editions when the great commercial crisis of 1586–87 was still fresh in men's minds. The West Country had been very badly affected in that event.

7. Printed as "clath" in the editions of 1590 and 1591.

8. Printed as "Spinsser" in the 1590 and 1591 editions.

9. "Emanuel," meaning "God with us," is put at the head of the letters given below, and presumably the young merchant was expected to follow this pious practice. Perhaps for that reason John Browne uses the supplication here.

10. The initials at the end of this remembrance are "T.A.," presumably standing for Thomas Aldworth. Thomas does not seem to have had an apprentice with the initials I.A., but he had a nephew John Aldworth, son of Richard Aldworth of London and brother of Robert Aldworth. John Aldworth was apprenticed to Thomas Saltern, grocer of Bristol, on 8 July 1566 (Bristol Record Office, *Apprenticeship Book 1566–1592*, fo. 119). In the edition of 1590 and later, the initials are given as "I.P.," not "I.A." This was probably a printer's error in the second edition, which was copied in later ones.

11. The opening paragraph in the 1589 edition differs in a number of ways from that used in later editions. The 1590 edition reads as follows: "A Generall remem-

brance for you my seruant I.P. that forasmuch as now it is my goodwil and determination to imploye you (by the grace of God) in trauaile beyond the seas: I doo thinke it therefore conuenient to recommend vnto your carefull obseruation, these fewe exhortations and instructions folowing. First, and principallie I doo earnestlie exhort you to have a most especiall care and regarde to the performance of your daylie of prayer and thankesgiuing to God: not omitting presentlie vpon your safe ariuall at your Porte, to render vnto God most hartie and humble thankes for his gracious protection of you, by saying as in token of your thankefulnes, some godlie prayer of thankesgiuing, or say onelie (with reuerence upon your knees) the *Lordes Prayer*, giuing him with all thankes in some words of your owne spirit".

12. In the editions of 1590 and later years, this phrase appears as "Secondly doo you remember, that presently vpon your ariuull at your Port: to make diligent inquirie. . . . "

13. Possibly the author felt that his advice about writing secretly was not in accordance with his expressed intention of benefitting the merchant community in general, and added this note by way of explanation.

14. The writer of *A Speciall Direction for Divers Trades*, c. 1575–85, stresses the importance of the merchant receiving "advertisements" from abroad, and remarks, "Therefore adverticement is good and the principall thinge that belongeth to A Merchaunte" (*Tudor Economic Documents*, edited by R. H. Tawney and Eileen Power, 1924, vol. III, pp. 207, 208).

15. The author seems to have considered this advice particularly important for a young man who would be active mainly in Spain and Portugal. It is repeated later in the letter. Englishmen engaged in the Spanish trade presumably regarded the Spanish in a different light than their countrymen did who were concerned with privateering.

16. The 1590 edition at this point runs: "Lastely (as I said vnto you in the beginning) let this bee your first and chiefest poynt. . . "

17. Kingroad is an anchorage at the mouth of the Avon, about 7 miles from Bristol.

18. The 1590 edition runs: "with my duetie also remembred to my good Mistresse, &c.".

19. "P.A." in the 1590 edition and later. Presumably a printer's error in 1590, copied in later editions. "R.A." probably stands for Robert Aldworth, nephew of Thomas Aldworth.

20. On 23 January 1593, letters of marque were granted to the *Gabriel*, 80 tons, master, William Furthe; owners, Thomas Aldworth, Robert Aldworth, and Edmund Browne (J. W. Damer Powell, *Bristol Privateers and Ships of War*, p. 48). As of 1 July 1594 there is a reference to a government subsidy paid to Thomas Aldworth and partners, merchants of Bristol, for their new ship, the *Gabriel* of Bristol, 105 tons (*Cal. S.P. Domestic*, 1591–94, p. 524). The *Minion* of Bristol, 250 tons, was one of the four Bristol ships taking part in the Armada campaign. The owner was John Satchfield (J. W. Damer Powell, *op cit.*, p. 48).

21. The word "impliments" is used to denote purchases by the factor.

22. "Stammels" referred to a coarse woollen cloth or linsey-woolsey, usually dyed red; "kersies" to a coarse narrow cloth made from long-staple combed wool; and "bayes" or baize to a fabric of fine texture introduced into England in the 16th century.

23. Not identified.

24. For the prices and measures given here, see *infra*, p. 19 ff.

25. The word "warrs" of this edition is corrected in later printings.

26. The phrase "my duetie also remembred" is employed in the 1590 edition.

27. "P.A." in the 1590 editions and later. See note 19.

28. The words "but they forced me . . . all" are omitted in later editions.

29. The words "the first pennie" are intended to give reference to the cost price before the various charges had been added.

30. A ship normally carried the goods of a number of merchants; and the various packets were marked with different marks and numbers for easy identification. There is an article on "Bristol Merchant Marks," with a great many illustrations, by A. E. Hudd in the *Proceedings of the Clifton Antiquarian Club*, Bristol, 1910–11, vol. VII, part II, pp. 97–194. The mark given in the text is presumably that of Thomas Aldworth. Merchants might use more than one mark, and, for another illustration of Aldworth's mark, see p. 47. In the 1590 edition, the mark used here was that of John Browne, as given below on p. 47. In the editions of 1616 and 1641, the mark used at this point is a key, presumably because the printer had such a device in stock, and did not want to go to the trouble of making special type.

31. The *Pleasure*, 150 tons, received letters of marque on 16 December 1592, owner, Thomas James. She may have been originally the *Mayflower*, which caught fire in Hungroad, but was recovered and repaired. She was one of the three Bristol ships fitted out for the Cadiz expedition of 1595 (J. W. Damer Powell, *op. cit.*, pp. 22, 25, 40, 42, 47).

32. See note 30 above.

33. "B.E." signifies bill of exchange.

34. "I.R." possibly refers to John Roberts, son-in-law of the author John Browne and brother-in-law to John Browne, Junior. John Roberts does not, however, seem in real life to have ever been connected with Robert Aldworth, who is given as the author of this letter. The *Toby* was a Bristol-built ship which received a government subsidy in 1590 (J. W. Damer Powell, *op. cit.*, p. 343).

35. The initials "P.R." presumably stood for the name of the draper, but I have not been able to identify him.

36. In the 1589 edition there is no merchant's mark in the margin as there is in later editions. The 1590 edition uses the mark of Thomas Aldworth, as given on p. 47.

37. In the 1589 edition, there is no merchant's mark in the margin. There is in the later editions, that of 1590 using the mark of John Browne.

38. John Barker was a prominent merchant of Bristol in the 16th century and early 17th century and, before the early editions of *The Avizo* became known, that work was sometimes attributed to him. He was sheriff 1593–94, mayor 1606–7, and died 13 September 1607. He was Assistant General of the Spanish Company in 1583; and his accounts for that year have survived. (See Patrick McGrath, *Records Relating to the Merchant Venturers of the City of Bristol in the Seventeenth Century*, p. XV and 1 ff.) John Barker was associated with Robert Aldworth and others in trade to Portugal in 1600.

39. "Pits" is probably an error for "Pitt." Thomas Pitt and Thomas Pitt, Junior, were members of the Spanish Company in 1605 (McGrath, *op. cit.*, p. 3).

40. There is some obscurity in this paragraph, which states that the Kintal is "100. li" but contains "102. li" English weight; nor is it clear how the Kintal of iron in Biscay which is 150 pounds makes but 114 pounds of English weight.

41. The "nail" is a measure of length for cloth, one sixteenth of a yard.

42. The word "his" appears instead of "the" before "Hannic," in the 1589 edition, a misprint which is corrected in later editions.

43. A misprint "a" appears in place of "and."

44. There is a printer's error at this point: the word "and" is repeated.

45. "Ode" means woad.

46. Train oil, obtained by boiling the blubber of whales, seals, and various fish.

47. The mark is used in the editions of 1589, 1590, 1591, and 1607. In 1616 and

1640 the printer used a different symbol, consisting of a "T" with a number of small lines. At other points, e.g., pp. 47 and 48, below, there were variations in the marks utilized in the various editions.

48. The nature of this duty has not been ascertained.

49. Foreigners were compelled to deal through an official broker.

50. "Aueredge" or "average" refers to any charge over and above the freight incurred in the shipping of goods, which is payable by their owner.

51. The "prouision" or "provision" is a commission payable to a factor.

52. The total is correct here, but in the 1591 edition it became oooM. 132 V. 506, owing to a printer's error.

53. This became oooM. 132.V.506 in the 1590 edition, and this error was copied in the 1591 edition.

54. It is not clear why "7. and a halfe" is suggested, unless commission was sometimes 7½ percent.

55. Given as "10 January 1589" in the editions of 1616 and 1640.

56. The practices of the several printers in the subsequent editions of *The Avizo* were the same at this point as at the preceding accounting form.

57. Given as "10 January 1589" in the 1616 and 1640 editions.

58. Given as "4 January 1589" in the 1616 and 1640 editions.

59. Given as "5 January 1589" in the 1616 and 1640 editions.

60. The phrase "per Kint Kats" appeared before "per Kintall" in the 1589 edition. It was eliminated in the 1590 and later editions.

61. Given as "10 December 1589" in the 1607 edition, and as "18 December 1589" in the 1616 and 1640 editions.

62. Possibly soaking them in water to make them sound before putting in the oil.

63. Presumably some kind of port due.

64. Perhaps some form of commission.

65. Making good the loss from leakage or absorption.

66. A Willian Megar was master of the *Aid*, one of the four Bristol ships in the Armada fleet, but there is of course no certainty that this is the man referred to here.

67. Apart from "Avizo" this is one of the very few Spanish words used in the work.

68. We might have expected "T.A." to be written here. Possibly "T.R." is a misprint.

69. Possibly John Barker (see note 38); perhaps John Browne.

70. This might possibly stand for Thomas James, sheriff, 1591–92, mayor of Bristol, 1605–6.

71. In the 1616 and 1640 editions, the mark in the margin is a key.

72. In the 1591 edition, this is followed by: "they paying the freite with auereges accustomed, according to the charterpartie."

73. The word "your" appears in this note in the 1589 edition, which is corrected to "you" in later ones.

74. The mark here in the 1590 edition is that of John Browne, as shown on p. 47. There is no mark in the 1616 edition, and in 1640 a curious symbol was used, consisting of a number of small lines not forming any recognisable initials.

75. The 1590 edition has here "marked as in the margent," and in the margin is the symbol of John Browne, as shown on p. 47.

76. The words "A bill of Exchange" are repeated in the margin of later editions; and succeeding five sub-headings are similarly handled.

77. The deep-water anchorage of Hungroad was about three miles down the Avon from Bristol Bridge.

78. The word "mored" becomes "mored and continued" in later editions.

79. In later editions a phrase of "to the assured his heires, executors and assignes" is introduced at this point.

80. The figure "15" appears in the text, but "25" in the tabulation at right.

81. In later editions there is a little hand in the margin pointing to each of the maxims.

82. In later editions this is followed by: "Rom. 16.21. To god onelie wise bee praise through Jesus Christ for ever. Amen."